JAZZ AND COMMERCIAL ARRANGING

Block Writing Techniques, Rhythm, and Melody

Andrew Charlton
California State, Fullerton

John M. DeVries

PRENTICE-HALL, INC., Englewood Cliffs, New Jersey 07632

Library of Congress cataloging in Publication Data

Charlton, Andrew.
   Jazz and commercial arranging.

   Contents: v. 1.–Block writing techniques,
rhythm, and melody – v. 2.–Accompaniment and
harmony.
   1.–Arrangement (music)   2.–Jazz Music–
Instruction and study.   3.–Improvisation (Music)
I.–DeVries, John M.   II.–Title.
MT68.C52   781.6'4   81-17758
ISBN   0-13-509869-6 (v. I)AACR2
ISBN   0-13-509893-9 (v. II)

To Donald Gunderson
A Superlative Jazz Educator

Printed in the United States of America

10 9 8 7 6 5 4 3 2 1

Editorial /production supervision
     and interior design by Barbara Alexander
Cover design by 20/20 Services, Inc.
Manufacturing buyer: Harry P. Baisley

ISBN 0-13-509869-6 {VOL. I}

PRENTICE-HALL INTERNATIONAL, INC., *London*
PRENTICE-HALL OF AUSTRALIA PTY. LIMITED, *Sydney*
PRENTICE-HALL OF CANADA, LTD., *Toronto*
PRENTICE-HALL OF INDIA PRIVATE LIMITED, *New Delhi*
PRENTICE-HALL OF JAPAN, INC., *Tokyo*
PRENTICE-HALL OF SOUTHEAST ASIA PTE. LTD., *Singapore*
WHITEHALL BOOKS LIMITED, *Wellington, New Zealand*

Contents

Part II

RHYTHM AND MELODY *69*

Preface

The most basic technique used in commercial music, from the many styles of jazz through the styles of Latin, country, blues, and yes, even in the many styles of rock, is what we call block writing. This technique involves paralleling a melody with a "block" of voices that contain the correct and essential chord tones producing a concerted and homogeneous sound.

Block writing is a common arranging device used for various instruments, whether they be saxophones, trumpets, trombones, strings, or any combination of like or unlike instruments. Even single instruments such as piano, organ, accordion and vibraphone can and often do use block techniques.

Part One of this book, therefore, deals with chord spellings, voicings, and part motion in general terms only, without delving into idiomatic considerations, and concentrating instead on the proper usage of block techniques applicable to all instruments including voices.

In commercial music, that is, music for use in the music industry—TV, radio, film, theater, stage acts, dance bands, and so on—block writing often forms the basis of harmonic treatment. A melody harmonized in block style sounds like a "sheet" of sound, totally natural and pleasing to the ear—the goal of most commercial music. Block writing is simple indeed, but does not intend to imply simplistic music or musical styles. Block writing is merely a satisfactory way of handling a melody with groups of instruments or voices.

The material in this book is designed for the beginning arranger to learn block writing in an organized manner. Extended chord spellings, modern notation, chord symbols; these are often new concepts to the musician who is not involved with commercial music. Clarification of terms and practices of commercial music are included in the text for those who have not had experience in commercial music, as well as for others who might benefit from a systematic approach to commercial arranging.

Open-block voicing is also explored in Part One, using four voices in all chord types through the dominant thirteenth. Scoring shortcuts are presented as a means of speeding up the learning process besides saving countless pencil strokes. By the end of Part One, the student will understand how to correctly harmonize a jazz-style melody in block voicing. Popular melodies in jazz style offer the easiest place to begin application of block voicing because of their rich variety of chord types. But remember, block voicing is a technique, not strictly a style. Although block voicing is extremely suitable to jazz styles, block application to other styles is not difficult if the style is understood in terms of harmony, melody and rhythm.

Teachers will find this book helpful because it is specifically designed as an introductory two-semester course in jazz and commercial arranging. Sufficient materials and examples are presented in each chapter so that students can master the skills necessary to handle each new concept. Included at the end of each chapter are "class exercises," intended for use by the students or to be done by the teacher, showing the correct way or ways to solve each problem. The class exercises provide a basis for questions, stimulate discussion, and are an invaluable tool necessary to understand and master each new practice. The worksheets at the end of this volume are intended as homework assignments; the teacher can use them to monitor each student's progress and as a basis for grading.

Whereas Part One of this volume deals with block writing, Part Two also uses block writing as its basis, with additional considerations being the rhythmic and melodic embellishment of a melody harmonized in block style. The rules and guidelines of Part One are put into practice in Part Two, the emphasis shifting from the simple filling in of voicings, to the development of experience, knowledge, and taste within various styles.

Part Two explores the techniques of rhythmic and melodic variation with harmonic variation not yet introduced, because, too often with inexperienced arrangers, interesting melodic invention is neglected at the expense of "wild" or "far out" harmonies and chord progressions. True, chord progressions and a thorough knowledge of harmony is important for altering and arranging a basic tune, but melodic interest is an equal, if not more important element.

The devices of variation developed in this volume are essentially the same ones that have been used for hundreds of years—rhythmic alteration, passing tones, single and double neighboring tones, and the use of other chord members. The only difference between the practices of, say, the sixteenth century and those employed in twentieth century commercial music, are simply stylistic in nature. The understanding of style, however, is difficult by simply reading about it in a book such as this, so the listening to and analysis of various styles of commercial music is highly recommended as both a classroom and individual activity.

Even though they may be far from definitive, the guidelines given in the text discussing rhythmic and melodic variation do offer principles that will help those students who have had little or no experience playing or listening to jazz and other types of commercial music and the articulation and embellishment proper to them. Although this volume is not intended primarily as a self-taught method, much can be gleaned from it by those who have had experience with commercial music as composers, arrangers, or performers.

The student who works through Volume One of JAZZ AND COMMERCIAL ARRANGING will be well on the way to a careful blending of the elements of the arranger's craft—creating a work in which there is a delicate balance of simplicity and sophistication, a careful blend of predictability and surprise, and above all, a smoothly flowing rhythmic and melodic idea.

ANDREW CHARLTON
JOHN M. DeVRIES

BLOCK WRITING TECHNIQUES
Part I

1

Chord Symbols
and Basic Chord Spellings

There seems to be a singular lack of standardization in the use and meaning of chord symbols used in commercial music. For instance, a minor seventh chord with a lowered fifth can in various systems be indicated by each of the following symbols:

Cmi7-5   Cm7-5   cmi7(-5)   Cmi.7(-5)   C-7-5   C∅   and even   E♭mi6/C

Because of the possible ambiguities inherent in the free use of all available symbols that are being or have been used, we will adopt a standardized, logical system, use only symbols that are truly musical symbols and remain consistent in its use.

A simple symbol indicating a major chord with no additional tones, in other words, a simple triad, is given as a root name:

A minor chord with no additional tones is indicated as follows:

Added sixths to either major or minor chords are indicated as follows:

3

For any symbol including the number "7," the word "minor" or "mi" applies only to the third of the chord, and the word "major" or "maj" applies only to the seventh:

Minor Seventh Chord

The "mi" tells us that the third is minor; the seventh is automatically minor; in other words, this is a minor triad with a minor seventh interval added above the root.

Major Seventh Chord

The "maj" tells us that the seventh is major; the third is automatically major; in other words, this is a major triad with a major seventh interval added above the root.

Seventh Chord

A seventh chord is automatically a dominant seventh chord, the third being major and the seventh being a minor seventh above the root.

Minor Major-Seventh

The "mi" indicates that the third is minor, whereas the "maj7" indicates that the seventh is a major seventh above the root.

Alterations, such as lowered or raised chord members, are notated inside parentheses. The only alterations allowed for now are the alterations of the fifth in the dominant chord (♭5 and ♯5) and the lowered fifth in the minor seventh chord (♭5). Also shown are raised and lowered fifths on the major seventh chord, although these are rather rare:

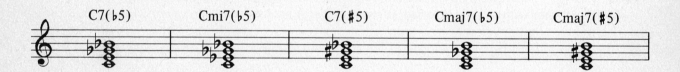

In commercial music, diminished chords are always full four-note structures built up of minor thirds. In actuality there are only three diminished chord sets (C-E♭-G♭-A, C♯-E-G-B♭, D-F-A♭-B); however, each inversion of the three is treated as if it were a different chord, always named from whichever tone is in the bass. Any convenient enharmonic spellings for these chords is acceptable, as there are no key-center implications with these chords:

Following is a listing of all usable chord types, with and without alterations, which have been covered so far:

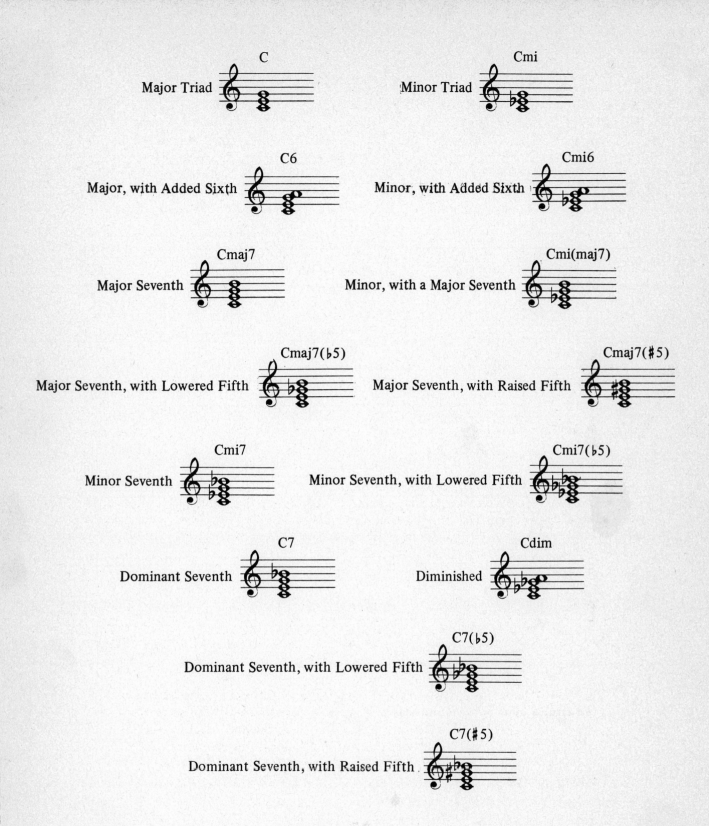

Major Triad — C

Minor Triad — Cmi

Major, with Added Sixth — C6

Minor, with Added Sixth — Cmi6

Major Seventh — Cmaj7

Minor, with a Major Seventh — Cmi(maj7)

Major Seventh, with Lowered Fifth — Cmaj7(♭5)

Major Seventh, with Raised Fifth — Cmaj7(♯5)

Minor Seventh — Cmi7

Minor Seventh, with Lowered Fifth — Cmi7(♭5)

Dominant Seventh — C7

Diminished — Cdim

Dominant Seventh, with Lowered Fifth — C7(♭5)

Dominant Seventh, with Raised Fifth — C7(♯5)

CLASS EXERCISES

Spell and notate correctly the following chords.

Assignment: Do Worksheets 1, 2, 3, and 4.

2

Closed-Block Voicing: Tonic Chords

In general, the most common and satisfactory way of harmonizing a melody in four voices is a rather simple structure called "block voicing." Closed-block voicing, as the name implies, is merely a "block" of voices with the melody in top; each voice below the melody takes the next available chord tone. A melody harmonized in closed-block voicing results in each of the lower parts being a melody of its own, paralleling the main melody in contour and rhythm.

Here are some important points concerning closed-block voicing:

1. The melody determines the rhythm, range, and contour of the remaining voices; all voices parallel the melody.

2. Use four different notes voiced from the melody down; do not duplicate or double notes.

3. Use only the root, third, fifth, and sixth or seventh for now; ninths, elevenths, and thirteenths will be added later, as they require special treatment.

4. Except for special effects, never voice the top two voices a half step apart, although half steps between any other adjacent voices are perfectly acceptable.

5. Because each chord must include four different notes, there will be no triadic structures; all major and minor chords must have an added tone, either the sixth or seventh.

For example, a four-part major chord with a C root may be either a C6 or a Cmaj7:

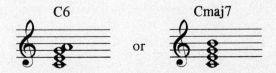

A tonic minor chord with a C root may be either a Cmi6 or a Cmi(maj7):

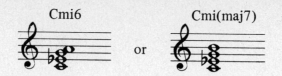

Sometimes the melody dictates the choice of either the sixth or major seventh, as in the following cases:

1. When the melody is the sixth, the chord is necessarily a sixth chord.
2. When the melody is the major seventh, the chord is necessarily a major seventh chord.
3. When the melody is the root, the next lower voice should not be the major seventh but, rather, the sixth so as to avoid the half-step clash between the top two voices.

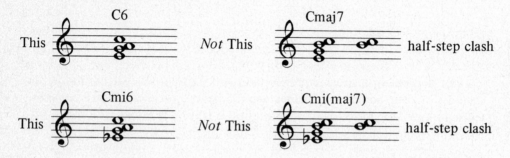

When the melody is the third or fifth of a major or minor triad, a choice must be made as to which is to be the added tone, either the sixth or the major seventh. Either can be correct, but consistent use of added sixths can result in a rather "dated" sound reminiscent of the 1940s, when the use of the major seventh in block writing was rare. Today the half-step clash between the major seventh and root is a desirable sound except between the top two voices. But still, with the emphasis on taste and variety, do not be afraid to sprinkle a few added sixths in a passage to relieve the possible monotony of continuous major sevenths.

Here are the possible harmonizations of a C chord using both the sixth and major-seventh in all positions or voicings:

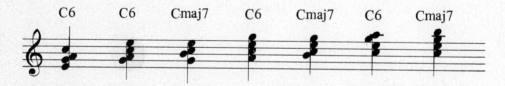

Following are the possible harmonizations of a C minor chord using both the sixth and major seventh in all positions or voicings:

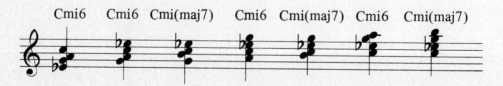

CLASS EXERCISES

Use additional manuscript paper to spell and notate the following chords in all voicings. Remember that a major or minor triad must have an added tone rather than being a simple triad. Remember also to avoid the half-step clash between the top two voices.

1. Eb	2. Gmi	3. D6
4. Ab6	5. Bbmi	6. Emi6
7. Ami(maj7)	8. Dmi6	9. Emi(maj7)
10. Abmi6	11. Gbmaj7	12. A
13. Fmaj7	14. Dbmi	15. Gbmi(maj7)

In the exercises be sure to spell the chords correctly in the implied tonality. In other words, the third of the Abmi6 chord is not B-natural but is C-flat. Later, when we deal with progressions of chords and have to consider voice motion in each part, we will then allow enharmonic equivalents when they make for more logical motion.

Remember also that a simple minor triad implies a minor tonality so that the added tones are either the sixth or major seventh, *not* the minor seventh, which implies a supertonic seventh function. There are some exceptions to this rule in certain types of modal structures; but for now, add the sixth or major seventh when the added tone is not indicated in the chord symbol.

Assignment: Do Worksheets 5 and 6.

3

Closed-Block Voicing: Varieties of Seventh Chords

The minor seventh, dominant seventh, and diminished chords present no special problems when the basic tones—root, third, fifth, and seventh—are in the melody: the remaining tones simply complete the voicing of the chord.

Here are the possible harmonizations for the remaining chord types covered so far (excluding altered chords):

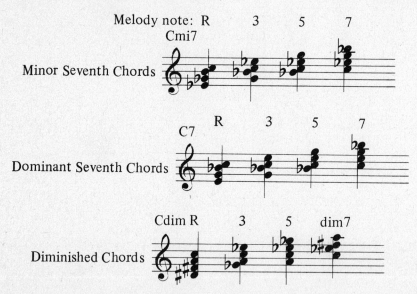

The minor seventh chord and dominant chord each have possible alterations of the fifth. The minor seventh chord uses a possible lowered fifth (♭5), and the dominant chord uses a possible lowered fifth (♭5) or raised fifth (♯5):

Voicing these altered chords—mi7(♭5), 7(♭5), and 7(♯5)—is exactly like voicing their unaltered form; just be sure to include the specified alteration in the chord block when writing closed-block voicing.

Keep in mind that closed-block voicing is the simultaneous writing of three distinct parts below a melody; therefore, accidentals must be added as required for each new voicing. Accidentals apply to one voice only, so be careful to check that each part is complete in itself—including all required accidentals.

When using closed block voicing, remember these important points:

1. Repeat accidentals to make each voice a line of music.
2. All voices are in close position; there are no duplicated tones.
3. Spell diminished chords in the most convenient way.
4. Minor seconds between adjacent voices are correct *except* between the top two voices.
5. Be aware of the key signature and any previous accidentals in a given measure.
6. Up to this point, closed-block voicing is simply changing the inversion of the given chord.

CLASS EXERCISES

Write closed-block voicings for the following chords using the indicated notes as the top voice.

Each of the following fragments contains at least one error. Identify and correct each of these.

Assignment: Do Worksheets 7 and 8.

11

Ninth Chords

Ninth chords must have five tones (R, 3, 5, 7, and 9) to be complete. Remember that the "maj" applies to the seventh and the "mi" applies to the third; therefore, a major ninth chord is a major seventh chord with an added ninth and a minor ninth chord is a minor seventh chord with an added ninth. Any alterations of fifths or ninths (or a major seventh added to a minor triad) must be parenthetical. Whereas minor ninth chords may have a lowered fifth (♭5) and dominant chords may have a raised ninth (♯9), lowered ninth (♭9), raised fifth (♯5), and lowered fifth (♭5), major and minor chords never use altered ninths.

Following is a listing of ninth chords including the most conventional alterations:

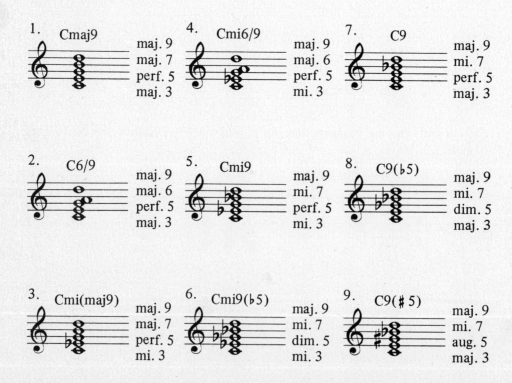

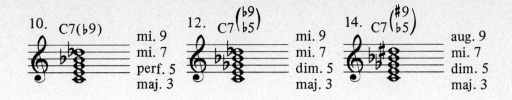

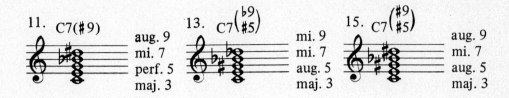

CLASS EXERCISES

The following list of chord symbols contain some that are incorrect according to the system we are using in this method. Identify and correct these.

1. C6

2. C#7 $\binom{\#9}{\#5}$

3. C7(#5)

4. F6(b5)

5. F7(b3)

6. Eb9

7. Emi7(b5)

8. Gb9 $\binom{\#9}{b5}$

9. B9(#5)

10. E(b9)

11. Bbmi(b9)

12. G(b9)

13. G9(b9)

14. F#mi(maj9)

15. Bmi7(b9)

16. Amaj7(9)

17. Abdim7

18. G#maj7(#9)

19. Dmi7(#9)

20. Bb9(b5)

21. Bb6/9

22. A7(maj9)

23. Ebdim

24. Dbmi6/9

Write the following chords in root position.

Dmaj9   Fmi(maj9)   Abmi9   Bmi9(b5)   C#9

E9(b5)   G9(#5)   Bb7(#9)   C7(b9)   Eb7 $\binom{b9}{\#5}$

F#7 $\binom{\#9}{\#5}$ A7 $\binom{b9}{\#5}$ Gb7 $\binom{\#9}{b5}$ Db6/9   G#mi6/9

Assignment: Do Worksheets 9 and 10.

5

Closed-Block Voicing: Unaltered Ninth Chords in Four Parts

As stated before, ninth chords must have five tones to be complete: R-3-5-7-9. Therefore, when voicing four parts in block style, we must omit one tone, and, with one exception, the omitted tone will be the root. Keep in mind that, in an ensemble with a rhythm section, the root need not be in the block voicing because it will be played by any or all of the rhythm section members—piano, bass, and guitar. Even if the rhythm section is tacit, the four-part closed-block voicing provides a definite and satisfactory key feeling adequate enough to make up for missing roots.

The one excpetion to omitting the root is when the root is the melody. Here the ninth is omitted, and the chord is thus treated as if it were a simple seventh chord. In other words, the seventh and ninth chords are interchangeable depending upon the melody note.

Voicings of the dominant ninth chord:

Melody note: R   9   3   5   7
C9

Voicings of the major ninth chord:

Melody note: R   9   3   5   7
Cmaj9

Note that in the major ninth chord when the root is in the melody, the chord is treated as if it were a C sixth, omitting both the seventh and ninth.

Voicings of the minor major-ninth chord:

Melody note: R   9   3   5   7
Cmi(maj9)

As in the major ninth chord, the minor major-ninth chord must omit both the seventh and ninth, including the sixth instead when the root is in the melody. Also, when the third is in the melody, the root must substitute for the ninth.

Voicings of the minor ninth chord:

Melody note: R   9   3   5   7
Cmi9

Note that the half-step interval between the top two voices with the third in the melody is avoided by omitting the ninth, making the chord a minor seventh. Also, when the root is in the melody, the chord is changed to a minor seventh.

Voicings of the major 6/9 chord:

Melody note: R   9   3   5   6
C6/9

Note that, when the root is in the melody, the ninth is omitted. In all other voicings, the ninth is substituted for the root and the sixth is substituted for the seventh.

Voicings of the minor 6/9 chord:

Melody note: R   9   3   5   6
Cmi6/9

As with the major 6/9 chord, the ninth substitutes for the root except when the third is in the melody because the half step between the top two voices must be avoided. The sixth replaces the seventh in this chord structure as in the major form.

Keep these principles in mind when using unaltered ninth chords in closed-block voicing:

1. One tone must be omitted—normally the root.

2. When the root is in the melody and cannot be omitted, leave out the ninth instead.

3. The ninth and minor third of a chord (half steps) cannot be in the top two voices. Change the ninth to the root.

4. If a ninth chord will not work in a given voicing, voice that chord as a simple seventh chord since seventh and ninth chords are interchangeable.

CLASS EXERCISES

Notate the following chords in all five voicings in four-part closed-block style.

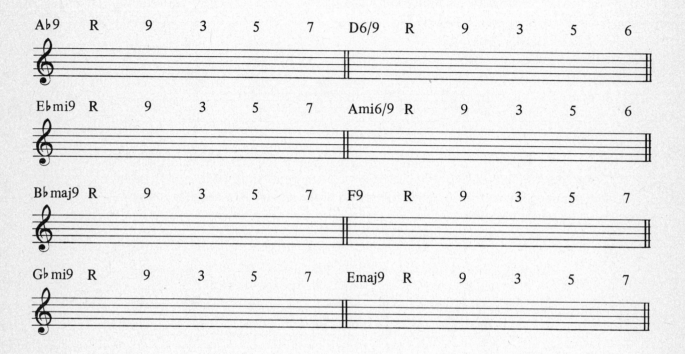

There are errors in some of the following examples. Identify the errors and correct them.

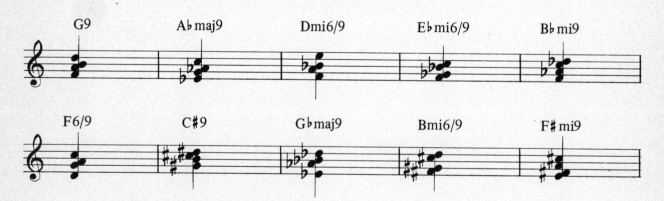

Assignment: Do Worksheets 11 and 12.

16

6

Closed-Block Voicing: Altered Ninth Chords in Four Parts

Some forms of altered ninth chords are handled in exactly the same way (with altered tones) as the unaltered forms. Others will require special treatment.

Chords requiring no special treatment:

When the root is in the melody, as in all six examples, there will be no ninth in the chord. In the minor ninth chord there is no ninth in the chord when the third is in the melody, avoiding the half-step clash between the top two voices.

Dominant chords with a raised ninth will be treated (for now) as if the only possible voicing is with the raised ninth in the melody:

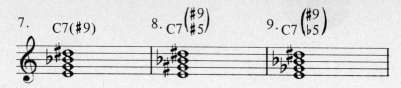

7. C7(♯9)   8. C7$\binom{♯9}{♯5}$ 9. C7$\binom{♯9}{♭5}$

Remember that ninth chords with alterations are invertible with the exceptions of the minor ninth chord with the third in the melody—the ninth being omitted—and any chord with a raised ninth.

CLASS EXERCISES

Notate the following chords in four-part closed-block style.

1. Melody note: Root

E7(♭9)   G7$\binom{♭9}{♭5}$ B♭mi9(♭5)   D7$\binom{♭9}{♯5}$ C♯9(♯5)   A♭7$\binom{♭9}{♯5}$ Fmi9(♭5)

2. Melody note: 9th or ♯9th or ♭9th

C7(♭9)   F♯7(♯9)   A9(♭5)   E♭7$\binom{♯9}{♭5}$ D7$\binom{♭9}{♭5}$ B♭7$\binom{♯9}{♯5}$ G9(♯5)

3. Melody note: 5th or ♯5th or ♭5th

E9(♯5)   A♭mi7(♭5)   D♭7$\binom{♭9}{♯5}$ F7(♭9)   Ami9(♭5)   G7(♭9)   B7$\binom{♭9}{♭5}$

4. Melody note: 3rd

B♭7$\binom{♭9}{♯5}$ C♭7(♭9)   D♭9(♭5)   E9(♯5)   F♯7(♭9)   G♯7$\binom{♭9}{♭5}$ Cmi9(♭5)

Idenitify and correct errors in the following examples.

Assignment: Do Worksheets 13, 14, and 15.

18

7

Melodies Harmonized in Four-Part Closed-Block Style

Harmonizing melodies in closed-block style is simply a matter of applying the techniques of inverting chords as we have been doing in the last few worksheets. There will be new considerations now as the harmonizations will have to parallel the melody rhythmically.

Study the following harmonized fragments carefully, noting how the lower voices parallel the melodies both in contour and rhythm:

EXAMPLE 1.

In the first measure the chord symbol reads simply "G." Analysis shows that various forms of a G major chord are used. The six chords in the first measure are actually G6, Gmaj7, G6, Gmaj9, G6 and Gmaj7. The effect to the ear is of G major tonality with added tones offering variety. The Bmi7(♭5) shows a simple series if inversions of the chord, and the E7(♭9) follows the practices that we have explored in the worksheets. What seems to be redundant use of accidentals in the second measure is not actually redundant when we realize that each line is a separate voice, as if four instruments were to play the passage, each reading their own line.

EXAMPLE 2.

As in Example 1, the first measure of Example 2 consists of various forms of the tonic chord, in this case Bb. Notice that, although the Eb9 chord is indicated on beat one of the second measure, it actually starts one-half beat earlier. Thus, when the melody is anticipated, the entire chord is also anticipated. The second Bb and the Fmi7 are also anticipated.

In both examples, there is no one absolutely correct way of harmonizing the tonic chords because of the many harmonizations that would be satisfactory using various tonic chord forms.

Let us now analyze a melodic fragment in terms of the possibiliities of harmonic treatment, remembering that choices will often have to be made among several equally correct ways of handling a given situation.

Remember also that, when a simple chord symbol such as F is given, it may be realized as any of the workable extensions of a major chord, namely, Fmaj7, F6, Fmaj9, or F6/9:

This melodic fragment is to be harmonized with an F major chord:

The first and last C, therefore can be harmonized in *any* of the following ways:

The G can be harmonized either of these ways:

And the A can be harmonized as shown:

Any combination of these will be considered correct, because all choices provide a good strong F major tonality.

Since a simple major chord symbol provides so much room for interpretation, the choice is really left to the arranger to include the additional tone or tones, be it the sixth, major seventh, major ninth or major ninth and sixth. A simple minor chord symbol such as Cmi offers the same extensions and additions as the major chord symbol C. The only difference is the minor tonality of the minor chord.

Listen carefully to the sound you prefer—especially to the half steps in the major seventh voicings and to the open sound of the 6/9 chord. Voice leading should also be considered when choosing voicings. Choose voicings that make each voice move whenever possible, avoiding the voicings that cause a voice to repeat a note while the melody moves. More will be said about voice leading later; for now simply use the voicings that you prefer and that work best.

Following are five different harmonizations of the fragment using various permutations of possible choices:

One choice is to use only major ninth chords:

Perfectly acceptable even though there is no root in the voicings.

Or to use only added sixths:

This has a 1940s sound. but it is certainly acceptable.

Or to use major sevenths but not ninths except where it is in the melody:

Nothing is wrong with this; it will sound good.

Or to harmonize only with F6/9:

Not the strongest of the choices, but it is not incorrect.

Or use all four possible chord types:

This offers a bit more variety, but it is not necessarily the strongest of the available choices.

In all the previous treatments of the melodic fragment, the chordal implication is of F major. If your harmonization uses predominantly the major seventh, or major ninth, or added sixth, or added 6/9, label the passage with the appropriate chord symbol. If, however, you use a mixture of two or more chord types, write the simplest symbol, in this case, F. It is not practical or desirable to write a different symbol every time the chord changes but yet is the same basic type. This would create a piano or guitar part unnecessarily complicated as the following:

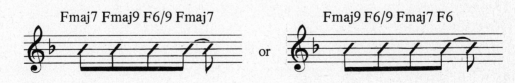

CLASS EXERCISES

Harmonize, making choices among the available types of tonic chords: sixth, major seventh, sixth and ninth, and major seventh and ninth.

Harmonize in closed-block style. Watch out for alterations in the chord that are not indicated in the chord symbol. These must be treated properly as altered chords.

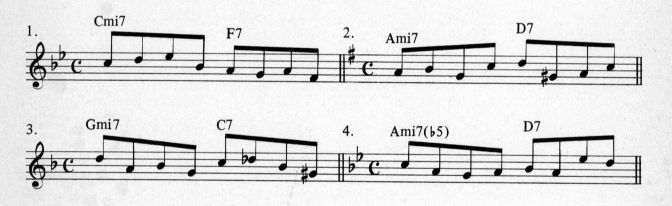

Assignment: Do Worksheets 16 and 17.

Anticipations

Rhythmic, melodic, and chordal anticipations, or where notes or chords occur earlier than expected, form the life essence of many commercial styles of music; this can certainly be true in the cases of the various jazz styles. It is important to fully understand the priniciples involved with the anticipation. These can take several forms:

Even though the A7 symbol is over the third beat of the measure, the actual A7 chord must be anticipated by a half beat. It is incorrect to harmonize the eighth note as an Emi7 and then change the chord to an A7 on the half note.

Even though the A7 symbol is indicated for the third beat, which is a rest, the eighth note must be treated as an anticipation and harmonized with the A7 chord.

There are two anticipations involved in this example:
(1) the first of the tied A's, which must be harmonized with the D7, and

(2) the final G, which must be harmonized with the G chord.

Avoid resolving chords on downbeats when they are anticipated with the melody as in the anticipated G in the following example:

A correct harmonization of this fragment must have the C6 chord anticipated on the last eighth note of the first measure:

The following incorrect example shows the C7 harmonized on the first beat of the second measure. If this were played by four instruments, it would sound as if the lower three instrumentalists were playing the passage incorrectly:

In other words, *anticipations must be in ALL voices.*

When writing four-part block harmonizations for a melody, remember that the three lower parts will usually parallel the upper part rhythmically, so that, when the melody has repeated notes, the lower parts will usually have repeated notes also. Often there may be some motion in the melody, but the under voices may have repeated notes. In the type of skeleton score we are doing, we can use a sort of "musical shorthand" as a time-saving device. Use slashes to indicate repeated notes in the lower parts:

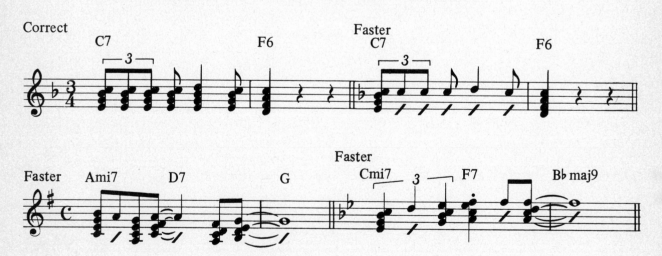

When the parts are extracted from the score, each must, of course, have the correct notes and rhythms filled in; that is, there must be no slashes in the individual parts.

CLASS EXERCISES

Harmonize the following fragments.

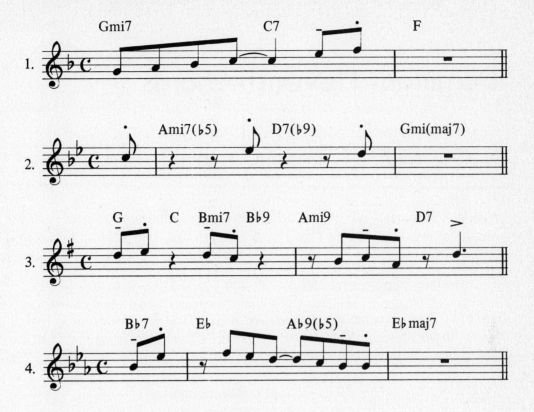

Assignment: Do Worksheets 18 and 19.

Dominant Eleventh Chords

Dominant eleventh chords are divided into two separate types: (1) chords with the unaltered eleventh, C11, and (2) chords with a raised eleventh, C9($\sharp$11). The unaltered eleventh variety requires special consideration because of the presence of both the eleventh and third, producing the harsh and undesirable minor ninth interval:

The chord shown, a full dominant eleventh chord, is not used in normal voicings because of its harsh sound. In actual practice, therefore, the third is omitted, leaving the fifth, seventh, ninth, and eleventh for usable tones in closed-block voicing.

Our usable C11 chord now becomes, in a sense, a Gmi7 with a C bass note (notated Gmi7/C) or a C9 with a fourth substituted for the third (notated C9sus4):

If we think of dominant eleventh chords as minor seventh chords over a different root (C11 = the Gmi7 chord over a C bass note), then it is easy to learn the voicings for the eleventh chord. In other words, think of an eleventh chord as a minor seventh with a root a fifth interval higher above the root of the original eleventh chord:

F11   becomes Cm7/F,

A$\flat$11 becomes E$\flat$mi7/A$\flat$,

$$B11 \quad \text{becomes } F\sharp \, mi7/B,$$
$$D11 \quad \text{becomes } Ami7/D, \text{ and so on.}$$

We can also use a minor ninth chord for the minor seventh chord, adding both variety and color:

$$E\flat 11 \quad \text{becomes } B\flat mi9/E\flat,$$
$$F\sharp 11 \quad \text{becomes } C\sharp mi9/F\sharp,$$
$$C11 \quad \text{becomes } Gmi9/C,$$
$$A11 \quad \text{becomes } Emi9/A, \text{ and so on.}$$

The following are voicings of the dominant eleventh chord. Remember that eleventh chords are voiced as minor seventh or minor ninth chords when used in four-part closed-block writing:

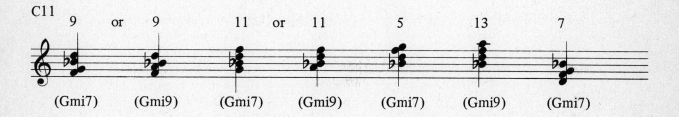

When the root is the melody, a minor seventh or minor ninth chord voicing is not possible, but two special voicings work nicely, one including the fifth and one including the ninth:

One other usable eleventh chord with the unaltered eleventh is the 11($\flat$9), an eleventh chord with a flatted ninth. This chord can be thought of as a mi7($\flat$5) chord for its closed-block voicings:

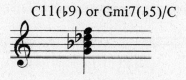

The 11($\flat$9) chord uses a mi7($\flat$5) chord built on the root a fifth interval higher than the original eleventh chord:

$$B\flat 11(\flat 9) \text{ becomes } Fmi7(\flat 5)/B\flat,$$
$$E11(\flat 9) \quad \text{becomes } Bmi7(\flat 5)/E,$$
$$G11(\flat 9) \quad \text{becomes } Dmi7(\flat 5)/G,$$
$$D\flat 11(\flat 9) \text{ becomes } A\flat mi7(\flat 5)/D\flat, \text{ and so on.}$$

The following are voicings of the 11(♭9) chord. As before, a mi9(♭5) may be used interchangeably with a mi7(♭5):

C11 (♭9)
R   ♭9 or ♭9   11 or 11   5   13   7

Other chords using an unaltered eleventh are (with a C root) the following:

C11(♯9)   C11(♯5)   C11 $\binom{♭9}{♯5}$ C11 $\binom{♯9}{♭5}$

C11(♭5)   C11 $\binom{♭9}{♭5}$ C11 $\binom{♯9}{♯5}$

The chords shown use alterations of the fifth and ninth in combination, and yes, we can use them in four-part closed-block voicings with certain limitations. But for now, we are limiting ourselves to the most conventional forms of the eleventh chord, and these forms are, with a C root, C11 and C11(♭9).

The dominant eleventh chord may be notated C11 or Gmi7/C or C9sus4. If you want to be absolutely specific about which notes to use in a dominant eleventh chord, avoid using the C11 symbol. Does C11 imply a full six-note structure with both the third and the eleventh present? Technically, yes; however, the dominant eleventh chord is more practical with the third omitted. Some arrangers may intend to imply *both* the third and the eleventh when using the C11 chord symbol, whereas others may assume that the C11 symbol omits the third automatically. To avoid such ambiguities altogether, the dominant eleventh chord is better notated as (with a C root) Gmi7/C, Gmi9/C, C9sus4; or Gmi7(♭5)/C or Gmi9(♭5)/C, in the case of a lowered ninth. When used in this method, the C11 symbol always implies omission of the third.

Dominant eleventh chords of the second type are those with alterations of the eleventh or raised eleventh (♭11 is meaningless). Here we will use the two most conventional variations of this type—9(♯11) and 7(♯11♭9)—leaving the other chord possibilities for open voicings in later chapters:

C9(♯11)   C7 $\binom{♯11}{♭9}$

To find the voicings for the chords shown, follow these steps:

1. Leave out the fifth.
2. Add the third and seventh.

3. Add the raised eleventh.

4. Add the ninth (not possible when the root is the melody).

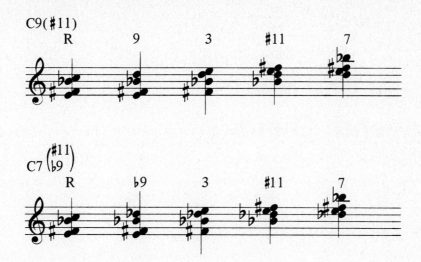

Since the raised eleventh is enharmonically equivalent to the lowered fifth, compare the voicings of C9(♯11) shown with the voicings of C9(♭5) and compare C7(♯11♭9) with C7(♭9♭5). The difference is purely visual, between G♭ and F♯; they are identical in sound.

CLASS EXERCISES

Voice the following in four-part closed-block.

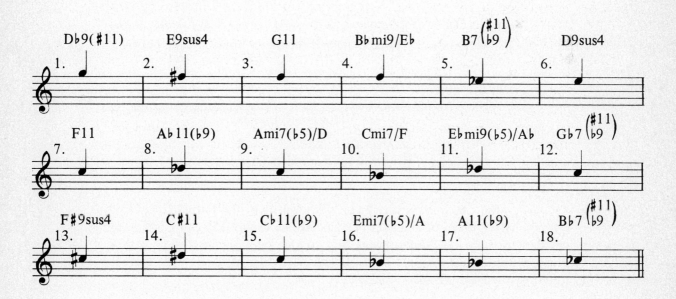

Assignment: Do Worksheets 20 and 21.

10

Major and Minor Eleventh Chords

A major chord with an added eleventh allows for only two possibilities: (1) the major ninth with a raised eleventh, maj9(♯11), and (2) the 6/9 with a raised eleventh, 6/9(♯11):

Cmaj9(♯11)   C6/9(♯11)

A major chord with an unaltered eleventh, as expressed in the chord symbol Cmaj11, is unacceptable because of the minor ninth interval between the third and the eleventh:

Cmaj11 (???)

Minor Ninth Interval

Since the raised eleventh (♯11) is equivalent to the flatted fifth (♭5), we can better think of Cmaj9(♯11) voicings as Cmaj9(♭5) and C6/9(♯11) voicings as C6/9(♭5). The voicings that follow are of major chords with a raised eleventh, but they are notated with flatted fifths to show the correct thinking when writing these voicings:

Cmaj9(♯11) or Cmaj9(♭5)

R   9   3   ♯11   5   7

C6/9(♯11) or C6/9(♭5)

Notice that, when (and if) the fifth is in the melody, the chord becomes a simple major ninth or 6/9 voicing. Also be aware that the maj9(♯11) and 6/9(♯11) chords are relatively rare and of limited usage, but they can be handled in closed-block in the voicings shown.

A minor eleventh chord is constructed by adding a minor third above the minor ninth chord. Unlike the dominant eleventh chord, however, the third of a minor eleventh chord is not omitted in its voicings.

The minor eleventh chord can be treated as if it were a minor seventh or minor ninth chord in all voicings except when the eleventh is in the melody:

Cmi11

Substituting Cmi7 or Cmi9 for Cmi11 makes the minor eleventh chord easier to handle than both the dominant eleventh chord and dominant ninth chord with a raised eleventh. Using the voicings just given, we see that a full six diatonic melody tones are harmonized with the minor eleventh chord.

The strict minor eleventh harmonization (always including the eleventh) may also be used, depending upon your individual taste, of course. The voicings presented now are also acceptable for a minor eleventh chord. Just be sure to include the third, seventh, and eleventh in each voicing, the additional tone being the root or fifth:

Cmi11

From these voicings we see that, in four-part closed-block, both the ninth and eleventh are not present in the same voicing (except when the ninth is in the melody). If there are more voices available, the voicings can include more chord members, but for now, because we are limiting ourselves to only four voices, we must always include the important chord tones, and then make logical choices as to which notes are left out.

CLASS EXERCISES

Write four-part closed-block voicings for the following melody notes.

Assignment: Do Worksheets 22 and 23.

11

Thirteenth Chords

Adding a third above the eleventh chord produces a thirteenth chord. As with the eleventh chord, some voicings of the thirteenth chord require special treatment, and with the exception of some of the altered forms of this chord, the eleventh will always be omitted. It is helpful to think of the thirteenth degree as a doubly raised fifth because in four-part writing, the fifth and thirteenth will never occur in the same voicing.

A thirteenth chord, C13, always implies a dominant function. Minor thirteenth and major thirteenth chords are theoretically possible but are better understood as minor ninth or major ninth chords with added tones. There is only one chord that *really* functions as a thirteenth chord and that is, of course, the dominant thirteenth.

When voicing unaltered thirteenth chords in closed-block style, follow these principles:

1. *Always* include the third and seventh.
2. *Never* include the eleventh (unless it is the raised eleventh).
3. Include the ninth and thirteenth whenever possible.
4. When the 5th is the melody, omit the thirteenth for a better sounding ninth chord.
5. Omit the root whenever possible.
6. When the root is the melody, omit the thirteenth for a less harsh seventh chord.
7. The thirteenth cannot be present when the seventh is the melody because the thirteenth and seventh would then produce half steps in the top two voices. Use a ninth chord instead.

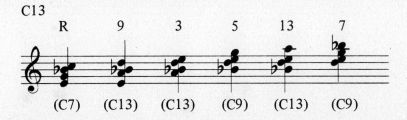

33

Study these voicings and note how the principles given are used to find a thirteenth chord voicing for each melody note.

Two altered forms of the thirteenth chord can be used in four-part block writing: the thirteenth with a raised eleventh, 13(♯11), and the thirteenth with a lowered ninth, 13(♭9):

Note how choices are made in these voicings as to which altered tones (♭9, ♯11) or extensions (9, 13) are included in each voicing. Be careful that these voicings are not used too low because of their high tension.

Further alterations with the thirteenth chord and other multiple alterations of the dominant chord are better used in five or more voices and in open voicings rather than in closed-block style.

CLASS EXERCISES

Voice the following in four-part closed-block. Some of these will be impossible to voice with a thirteenth in the structure; write the appropriate voicing and relabel the chord if needed.

Assignment: Do Worksheets 24 and 25.

12

Additions to the Diminished Chord

Tones are often added to the diminished chord that function as appoggiaturas but unlike the appoggiatura *need not* resolve to the tone over which they are suspended. At a casual glance these may "look" wrong, but they are actually the result of a very common practice. The added tone or tones are a whole step above a normal tone in the diminished chord. See, for instance, the following:

In this fragment the B is not a note in the E♭dim chord but is actually an appoggiatura over the chord member A.

Therefore, the block harmonization of this example is the following:

In four-part writing, treat the added tone as replacing the nearest lower chord member. Note that, in voicing the diminished chord with the appoggiatura, B is not next to the note that it replaces, although that note, A, could be voiced an octave lower if there were five or more voices.

Added-tone diminished chords often (but not always) use symbols with the appoggiatura note indicated in parenthesis:

If, however, there is no parenthetical addition to the diminished chord symbol and the note to be harmonized is obviously not part of the chord, but is a whole step above *any* of the chord tones, treat it as an appoggiatura.

Here are the single-addition varieties of the Cdim chord:

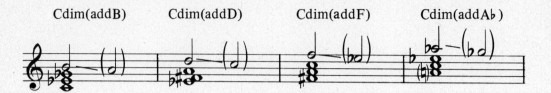

Notice that the possible added tones (B-D-F-Ab) form another diminished chord one step higher than the original diminished chord.

It is also possible to have *two* added tones in four-part block:

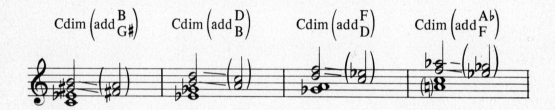

CLASS EXERCISES

Notate the following in four-part closed-block style. Use the added tone or tones in the top voice or voices only.

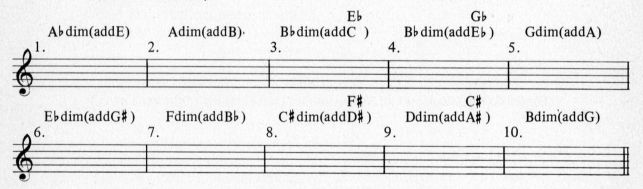

Complete the following using half notes for the lower parts.

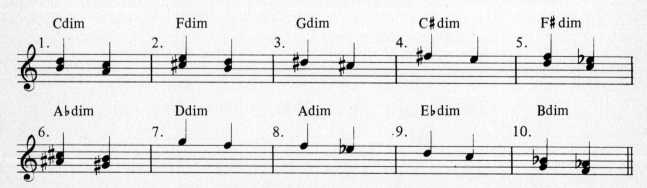

Assignment: Do Worksheets 26 and 27.

13

Melodic Nonchordal Tones: The Diminished Harmonization in Major Chords

Up to now we have covered in detail the handling of only chord members as melody notes in four-part closed-block style. But actual melodies, as we know, rarely limit themselves to pure chord tones without at least occasional passing or auxiliary tones. For example:

The third note, F, in this fragment cannot be harmonized by a C major structure using any of the techniques covered up to this point.

Nonchordal tones (and even some tones that are chordal) will be handled in one of three ways, the best depending upon smooth movement of voices:

1. Diminished chords
2. Diatonic chords
3. Parallel neighboring chords (the half-step shift)

The diminished chord solution is often good because of the nontonal character of the symmetrical diminished structure. Think of a melodic nonchordal tone as a chord member of a diminished chord and complete the diminished voicing by adding three voices below the melody. Sandwiched between chord tone voicings, the diminished chord voicing usually provides for movement in all voices and sounds fine as well.

Following is a harmonized melody using several neighboring and passing diminished chords. The nonchordal diminished chords are marked with an "X":

Play each of the four voices individually, noting how smoothly each line moves. When the melody is in motion, all the voices are also in motion. Motion in all parts is the goal of using diminished chord harmonizations.

Here is the way in which we have been harmonizing a scale (excluding the fourth degree):

Notice that in the harmonization shown there are times when two or more voices remain motionless. While the harmonization is technically correct, the lower parts would sound awkward when played, so situations like this should be avoided in favor of motion in all parts.

Here is a harmonization of the previous passage using diminished passing chords. The basic chord feel is of a G6:

The diminished chord voicing can occur on accented beats as long as it moves quickly to a chord containing the principal tonality, but it is important not to dwell too long on what is essentially a passing chord. There are occasions when it is impossible to move all voices, forcing a tone or tones to be repeated:

In the correct version given, the second chord must be treated within the C tonality because of its relative long duration in its context. The lower voices *must*, therefore, be repeated.

Depending upon context, chord tones (especially the 6, 7, 9, 11, and 13) may be harmonized with diminished chords when they connect the basic chord members R, 3, and 5. The important thing to keep in mind is the smooth motion in all parts.

The following is an F major scale using diminished chord harmonizations on chord tones as well as on nonchordal tones:

Notice how in the example the D, E, F, and G are harmonized by chord tones or by diminished chords, depending upon context. While it is possible to use diminished chords for both chord and nonchordal tones, be careful when applying this technique to melodies. Stay with the chord tone harmonizations as much as possible.

For instance, the previous example sounds good used with the following rhythm because most of the important notes (held notes, anticipations, and downbeats) are harmonized with chord tones:

CLASS EXERCISES

Harmonize the following fragments. Use diminished chord voicings if needed to avoid repeated notes in the lower parts.

Assignment: Do Worksheets 28 and 29.

14

Melodic Nonchordal Tones:
The Diminished Harmonization
in Varieties of Chords

Diminished chords can also be used with dominant harmonizations. Following is a C scale harmonized with a G7 chord:

Notice how certain chord tones (9, 13, and even the root!) in this example are harmonized with a diminished chord. Follow each voice and see how logically and smoothly it moves.

Minor seventh and minor ninth harmonizations:

The F♯ should not be harmonized with a diminished chord because this progression is weak; however, there is a diatonic structure that works quite well and that we will explore soon.

Tonic minor harmonizations:

As with the minor seventh chord passage, the F♯ should not be harmonized with a diminished chord.

Occasionally two neighboring tones must be harmonized between normal chord tones:

In each of these examples the first and fourth chord is what the ear hears; the neighboring tone harmonizations are heard as neutral chords bridging the principal chord structures.

Do not leap *from* a nonchordal structure:

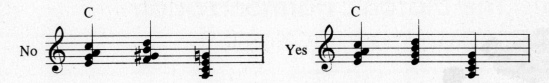

In the example the repeated notes are simply unavoidable in the second chord.

It is, however, perfectly acceptable to leap *to* one of these chords:

The important consideration in using any of the nonchordal harmonizations is the motion *away* from the nonchordal harmonization, *not* the motion to it. A nonchordal harmonization must resolve smoothly to a chordal structure, not leap to it.

CLASS EXERCISES

Harmonize the following fragments.

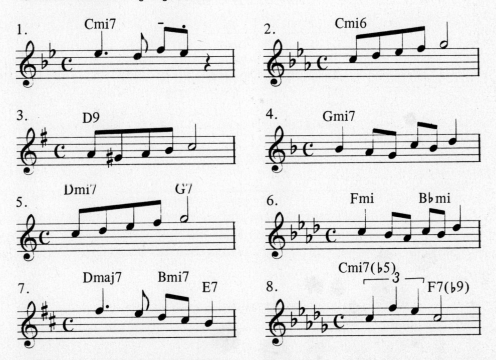

Assignment: Do Worksheets 30 and 31.

15

Melodic Nonchordal Tones: The Diatonic Harmonization

The purpose of diatonic auxiliary and passing chords is to harmonize nonchordal tones smoothly with no repeated notes in the lower parts. Unlike diminished chords, which may provide voicings for all nonchordal tones, diatonic and chromatic tones alike, diatonic chords may be used only when the melody note is diatonic to the key or temporary key area as indicated by the chord symbols.

To find a diatonic chord voicing, first establish the "type" of chord under which the nonchordal tone is to be harmonized—either I, II, or V. Following are all chord types covered so far in each of their respective categories:

KEY OF C MAJOR

I	II	V
C	Dmi7	G7
Cmaj7	Dmi9	G9
Cmaj9(♯11)	Dmi11	G11
C6		G13
C6/9		
C6/9(♯11)		

KEY OF C MINOR

I	II	V
Cmi	Dmi7(♭5)	G7(♭5)
Cmi(maj7)	Dmi9(♭5)	G7(♯5)
Cmi(maj9)	Dmi11(♭5)	G7(♭9)
Cmi6		etc. (any altered
Cmi6/9		dominant)

OTHERS (diminished)

Cdim
Cdim(add B)
Cdim(add B, G♯)

Simply put,

> major, minor sixth, minor-major seventh chords are I,
>
> minor sevenths are   II,
>
> and dominant chords are   V.

For a melody note harmonized by a major or tonic minor chord (I), choose a voicing from the other two related categories (II or V). For a melody note harmonized by a minor seventh, minor ninth, or minor eleventh chord, choose a related I or V; for a harmonized dominant chord (V), choose a related I or II. In other words, if the first and third notes are harmonized by a major chord, the second note is harmonized by either a related II or V:

If the first and third notes are harmonized by minor seventh, minor ninth, or minor eleventh chords, the second note is harmonized by either a related I or V:

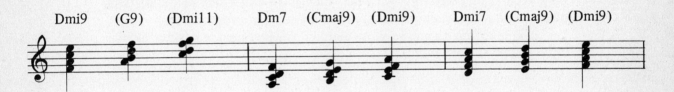

If the first and third notes are harmonized by a dominant chord, the second note is harmonized by the relative I:

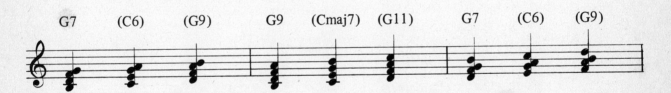

The most practical and common nonchordal diatonic voicings are those that use only the chords shown:

C MAJOR			C MINOR		
I	II	V	I	II	V
C6	Dmi7	G9	Cmi6	Dmi7(♭5)	G7(♭9)
Cmaj7	Dmi9		Cmi(maj7)	Dmi9(♭5)	
Cmaj9			Cmi(maj9)		

Notice that a plain dominant seventh chord (G7) is not in the table. This is because a simple seventh chord used as a diatonic nonchordal voicing sounds too plain and sometimes sounds "wrong." Use the dominant ninth form (G9) instead. When the 7(♭9) form is used—G7(♭9)—notice that the voicing is actually a diminished chord.

The B in this fragment cannot be harmonized with a Dmi7 chord (B is not a chord tone), and a diminished passing chord is weak because of two repeated notes:

Since Dmi7 is a II chord, we use a form of I (C6, Cmaj7, or Cmaj9); or we use V (G9). The only solution finally possible allowing voice motion in all parts is the Cmaj9 voicing shown now:

Notice that the Cmaj9 voicing forces the third melody note to be harmonized with a minor ninth chord voicing, allowing all voices to move. We may experiment, therefore, with the voicings on either side of the diatonic chord, trying to find a workable solution for complete voice motion.

The following examples show diatonic voicings used as passing, auxillary, and appoggiatura chords:

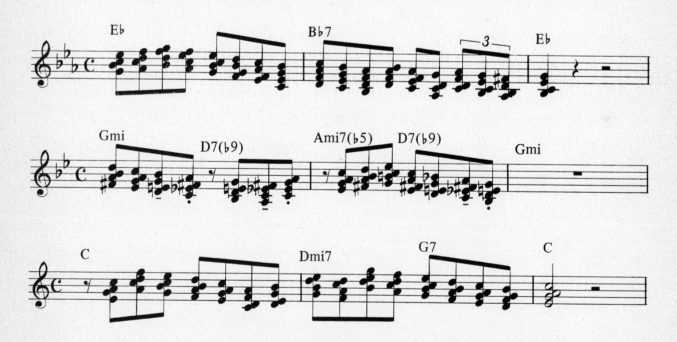

If a diatonic chord solution that allows motion in all parts is not found after trying all the possible voicings and using different voicings for the surrounding chords, we are forced into a diminished chord voicing or the half-step shift, which is discussed in the next chapter.

44

CLASS EXERCISES

Identify the related I or II or V for each of the chords following that can be used for diatonic nonchordal harmonizations. For example,

    1. Ab maj7 uses Bb mi7, Bb mi9, or Eb 9.

    2. Bb mi uses Cmi7(b5), Cmi9(b5), or F7(b9).

1. Cmi	2. Dmi7	3. F13	4. Ab maj9
5. B11	6. A6/9	7. Eb mi9	8. Gb maj9
9. C#13	10. Emi11	11. C7	12. Bb dim
13. F# mi7(b5)	14. D9(#11)	15. Db maj7	16. Gmi

Voice the following three-note fragments using diatonic harmonizations to avoid repeated notes in the lower parts.

Assignment: Do Worksheets 32 and 33.

16

Melodic Nonchordal Tones: The Half-Step Shift

A tone that approaches a chord tone by half step from above or below can be harmonized simply by shifting the entire chord tone voicing up or down. This half-step shift makes for very smooth motion—all parts move by half step up or down:

The second note B can be harmonized by a diminished chord, but using the half-step shift creates even smoother voice motion. Using this device, *any* chord can move a half step in either direction as long as it returns to the normal chord structure before passing on.

A scoring shortcut used frequently with the half-step shift is the use of angled dashes leading up to or down to a normally harmonized melody note. The dashes are understood to mean half-step motion:

As you can see, scoring is considerably simpler, faster, and less cluttered by using dashes to cut out the numerous accidentals necessary when notating half steps. Of course, when instrumental parts are copied from a score using dashes, each part must be complete, with all notes filled in—no dashes may be used in individual parts!

It is possible to leap *to* a half-step shift situation:

But do not leap *away* from a half-step shifted chord. As with other forms of nonharmonic chords, the important consideration is the motion toward a principal chord, not how you leave it.

And it is possible to begin the half-step shift on an accented beat:

The half-step shift may be used anytime a chord tone is approached by half step, even if both tones are chord tones:

The important thing to keep in mind is, that *the half-step shift must resolve to its correct position before proceeding.* In other words, do not shift *away* from a normal voicing immediately to another harmony, but shift *to* a normal voicing before going on to other harmonies.

The following examples illustrate faulty use of the half-step shift with their corrected versions:

It is also possible to use the half-step shift two or more times in succession. First, write the voicing of the normally harmonized chord tone; then, "back up" the entire voicing as far as needed:

CLASS EXERCISES

Harmonize each fragment two ways; use only chord tone harmonizations and the half-step shift.

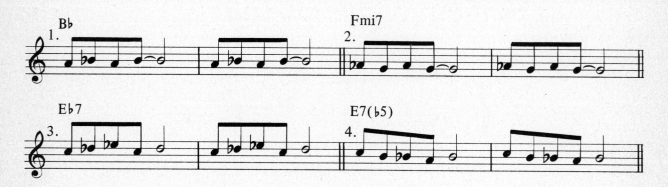

Correct the following errors involving the half-step shift.

Harmonize, using the half-step shift correctly.

Assignment: Do Worksheets 34, 35, and 36.

48

17

Four-Part Block Voicing: Instrumental Considerations

Until now, we have harmonized fragments with only one thing in mind—the correct voicing of melodies using various chord structures. While we have been careful to have the lower parts in motion when the melody also moved, the exercises have been mainly theoretical so far, apart from playing them at the piano. These previous exercises would sound quite good, however, if they were transcribed for combinations of instruments such as trumpets, trombones, saxophones, or other instruments; each part being a separate melody with a character of its own, each part important to the effect of the whole ensemble.

When writing for instruments, some obvious fundamentals must be understood. Range, timbre, relative weight, and flexibility as well as transposition and notational conventions are all elements that must be considered.

Shown now are ranges and transpositions for instruments commonly used in commercial music:

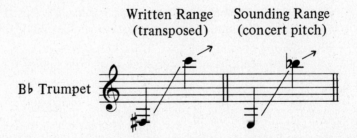

Trumpet parts are always written in treble clef and must be transposed a major second higher, adding two sharps to the key signature or subtracting two flats.

The trombone employs the bass clef principally, less often the tenor and alto clefs. It is a nontransposing instrument sounding exactly where written and not as agile, generally, as the trumpet or saxophone.

All members of the saxophone family have the same written range and use only the treble clef:

The written range of the saxophone family (without extension keys) is:

The transposed ranges of the saxophone family is:

Many saxophones are now made with high F♯ keys, which push the possible range up a half step, and many baritones are now made with low A keys, which sound low C.

The following transposition chart for saxophones must be memorized:

INSTRUMENT	TRANSPOSITION (from concert pitch)
Soprano saxophone	Up a major second (add two sharps to the key signature)
Alto saxophone	Up a major sixth (add three sharps)
Tenor saxophone	Up a major ninth (add two sharps)
Baritone saxophone	Up an octave and a major sixth (add three sharps)

When transposing from a concert sketch to parts that are played by instruments, it is often necessary to use enharmonic changes to make those parts logical for the instrumentalists. In other words, each part must be a clear, melodic line of music. Certain intervals and passages should be altered to achieve this end.

Avoid augmented seconds and diminished thirds unless the contour demands it:

50

Avoid diminished fourths and augmented thirds unless the contour demands it:

Avoid diminished sevenths unless they resolve inward:

Nothing is wrong with using double flats or double sharps if they make a passage clearer:

Do not contradict the key
signature; use it correctly
to avoid ambiguities:

No

Above all, apply logic and common sense:

CLASS EXERCISES

Based on the ranges given for the trumpet, trombone, and the saxophone family, how
many of these instruments can play each note shown?

1.   2.   3.   4.   5.   6.   7.   8.   9.   10. 11. 12. 13. 14. 15. 16.

Transpose the following for the parts indicated; provide correct key signatures for each
part; make each part logical. Write the trumpet and alto and tenor saxes in the original
octave; write the baritone sax one octave lower.

52

Assignment: Use Worksheets 37 and 38 to transpose the following chorus for, from top voice to bottom voice, trumpet, alto saxophone, tenor saxophone, and trombone. Make each part logical and without ambiguities. Be sure to have the correct key signature at the beginning of each line. All phrase markings and articulations must be in each part.

FOUR-PART BLOCK BLUES

Andrew Charlton
John M. DeVries

18

Special Part Writing and Harmonic Considerations

In block writing, all parts need not always follow the exact rhythm of the melody. Occasionally it is better to allow the lower parts to sustain while the melody moves. Two instances in which this is more satisfactory is when the fifth (with the thirteenth) or ninth (with the root) are in motion in the melody:

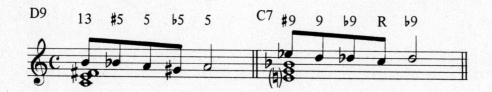

Sustaining the lower voices is preferable to having them repeat in eighth notes with the melody, and is an alternative to using the half-step shift or other devices.

An important consideration in deciding whether or not to sustain the lower parts is the logical motion and rhythm of those parts. Study the following examples, noting how possible lower parts can be improved:

The second version is better than the first because each voice moves with the melody. In the first example, the rhythm of the lower parts is rather awkward.

In the best example that follows, diminished chords on the thirteenth degree make for very smooth voice motion:

Following is a fragment using a fairly standard harmonization:

Once again, using diminished chords for the third and fifth structures allows each voice to move smoothly—but here is a different possibility:

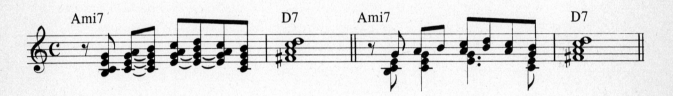

Notice how each voice has a character of its own, the lower voices both sustaining and moving.

The individual parts of the example just shown transposed for a quartet of saxophones appear this way:

Notice that tenuto marks and slurs are used in the transposed parts. Use tenuto marks when one or more parts have eighth notes while other parts have quarter notes; this ensures that sustained parts are held for full value and are not "clipped" as might be the natural tendency in a jazz style.

In the previous example, not only do the lower voices sustain, but, when the eleventh is in the melody, the ninth is the second voice and there is no third in the chord at that moment! The eleventh and ninth are double appoggiaturas, tones over the third and root, respectively. This structure is acceptable as long as the appoggiaturas resolve to their proper tones before proceeding. In other words, this can be correct:

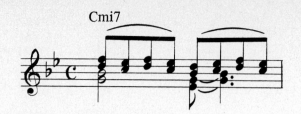

Cmi7

Analyze this carefully noting that the minor seventh chord actually occurs only on the resolution of the two appoggiaturas.

Thus, as can be seen, when the melody moves from the eleventh to the third in a minor seventh chord, the ninth can move to the root. This is a desirable usage whenever possible.

Sometimes the melody is static while the chord symbols indicate motion in the lower voices:

C   Fmaj7 Bbmaj7 Eb6   Dbmaj7   Ab6

The important principle here is the following: when the melody is static and the harmony changes, avoid repeating notes in the lower parts. When the voicings are completed, add ties where repeated notes occur.

Do not, however, copy the parts with ties, but edit each part from the score, being careful to notate each part correctly, using slurs when the lower parts move while the melody is sustained.

Shown now are the three lower parts of the previous example copied correctly and transposed for three trumpets:

Trumpet 2   Trumpet 3   Trumpet 4

CLASS EXERCISES

Harmonize, using sustaining lower parts where possible.

Harmonize, using the special application of the appoggiatura on the minor seventh chord and sustaining the lower parts on all chords wherever possible.

Assignment: Choose one or several of the leadsheets from Appendix 1; arrange, copy parts, and play.

19

Four-Part Open-Block Voicing

The most commonly used type of four-part open-block voicing is achieved by displacing the second voice from the top in a close-block structure down an octave. Simply moving the second voice down an octave results in a richer and fuller sound, particularly when the melody is in a rather high register. In general, open-block voicing can be used with any of the chords and voicings that have been covered so far:

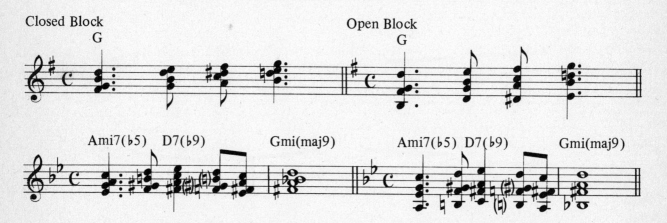

Be careful when using open voicing if the chord is a sixth chord with the root in the melody. The second voice is the sixth, and this voice placed down an octave results in a strong sounding minor seventh chord, the root of the minor seventh chord in the lowest voice, for example:

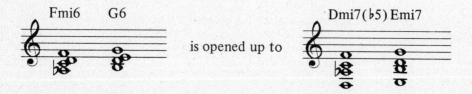

These voicings would be less of a problem if the chords were an octave higher, but in the octave indicated they are very ambiguous. In the range shown, the chords should be voiced in close position unless passed by quickly.

A desirable way in which to use open-block voicing is to alternate from open to closed position, depending on the melodic contours:

Notice how we have planned our voicings: when the melody lies low in the staff, the voicings are closed; when the melody lies higher in the staff, the voicings are open. There are no strict rules governing the use of either of these voicings—this and other examples could be harmonized using either closed or open block throughout. But using both voicings in juxtaposition offers a more smooth and satisfactory result.

Here is a harmonization of the last fragment using the open-closed scheme:

Following is the fragment just shown transposed for two trumpets and two trombones:

Trombone 2

CLASS EXERCISES

Write block voicings for the following fragments using open or closed position where desirable.

Assignment: Choose a leadsheet from Appendix 1 and arrange, using logical combinations of open- and closed-block voicing. Copy parts and play.

20

Four-Part Block: Independent Inner Voice Motion

With open-block voicing now introduced, two open voicings now become desirable over the closed position. Both are forms of the dominant chord with the root in the melody. The closed position voicings are shown now:

These chords are used better in open voicing (if possible) because the ambiguous whole-tone cluster in G7(♯5) is clarified in open voicing and the G7 offers a desirable usage of the thirteenth (doubly raised fifth):

Even if the chord symbol does not specify the thirteenth, the inclusion of the thirteenth in the voicing given is perfectly acceptable and pleasing.

Dominant seventh chords that have no specified alterations may use voices moving through alterations of the fifth and ninth to provide variety and added interest. While one or more voices move independently among usable alterations, the remaining voices may be static, repeating, or in restricted motion:

The following are examples of dominant chords showing independent inner voice motion using altered fifths and ninths. Inner voice motion is not restricted to the descending chromatic passage as illustrated, but may be any logical, musical, and correct melodic and rhythmic permutation of the alterations given.

When the melody is the root, lowered ninth, ninth, or raised ninth, the fifth is movable:

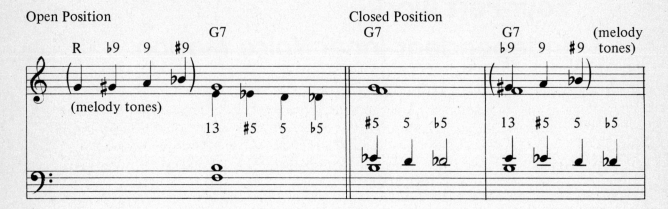

When the melody is the third or seventh, the fifth or ninth, or both are movable:

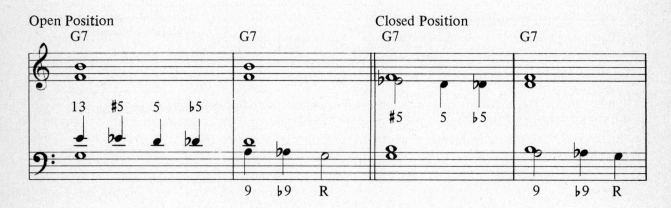

When the melody is the lowered fifth, fifth, raised fifth, or thirteenth, the ninth is movable:

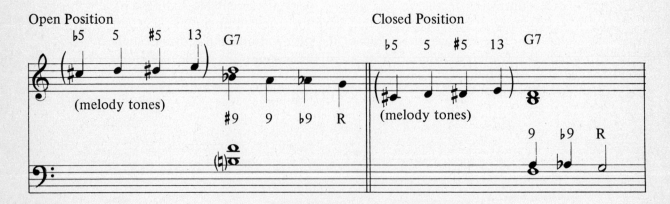

Think of melody notes in dominant chords as part of a chromatic scale when using independent inner voices:

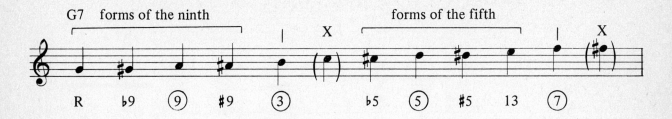

Notice that the root can be thought of as a doubly lowered ninth in the same way the thirteenth is thought of as a doubly raised fifth.

Also notice that we have not used the two melody notes C and F♯ (the eleventh and major seventh) in G7 voicings with independent inner voices. The major seventh melody note in a dominant chord is almost always voiced with the half-step shift, and apart from a flatted ninth, the eleventh melody note is better voiced unaltered.

Minor seventh chords use motion between 9-root and 11-3:

The mi7(♭5) and mi9(♭5) chords are used exactly as the mi7 and mi9, the only difference being the flatted fifth.

Major and tonic minor chords use motion between 9-root and 7-6:

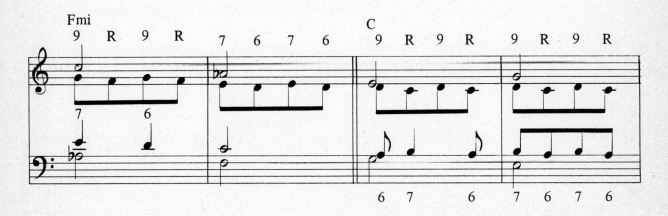

Diminished chords may use appoggiaturas in inner voices:

Occasionally, half-steps may be allowed between the the top two voices when the second voice is in motion *if* the half steps are not articulated together and they resolve to a normal voicing before going on to a new voicing. The same prinicples must be applied when open voicing is used; that is, when the half step becomes a minor ninth interval:

Chromatic passing tones may be used to connect diatonic tones or appoggiaturas in various chord structures:

Do not, however, use chromatic neighboring tones unless they are also chord tones such as alterations of the fifth or ninth:

Remember that, when the melody is anticipated, all other voices must also be anticipated. Therefore, an important consideration when using independent inner voice motion is the correct handling of anticipations and articulations in the melody. Be sure that independent inner voices arrive at anticipations and articulations *simultaneously* with the melody, not before or after:

Following are fragments illustrating correct and desirable usage of independent inner voice motion in closed-block and open-block voicing:

CLASS EXERCISES

Complete the block voicing for the following fragments using combinations of open and closed position. Use independent lower voice motion wherever possible.

18.

Assignment: Choose several leadsheets from Appendix 1 and arrange, using open- and closed-block voicing and independent motion in inner parts where desirable. Copy parts and play.

RHYTHM AND MELODY

Part II

21

Rhythmic and Articulation Considerations in Jazz and Commercial Music

The rhythmic treatment of melodies could well fill many volumes with concepts and practices. What is presented in the next few chapters is by no means exhaustive; but it is intended to be practical, simple, and immediately usable. While the alteration and embellishment of melodies should not be done according to strict unbreakable rules, there are guidelines nevertheless that have developed in jazz and commercial music that can be used to avoid awkward-sounding passages. The first elements that we shall explore are articulation and rhythmic variation.

In general, leadsheets are rhythmically simple, rarely employing rhythms that "swing" or are interesting in a jazz sense. We must, therefore, alter those basic rhythms to make them conform to the desired style of an arrangement. By the end of this volume you should begin to develop a sense of direction in your use of rhythms and articulations, a sense of continuity, logic, interest, and, above all, good taste.

Good taste, of course, cannot be taught, but it can be learned by careful and selective listening, keeping the ears open to many styles of music. When you hear something particularly pleasing, analyze what is happening; find out how a particular effect is achieved and, more important, how to notate specific passages. Understanding the principles of rhythmic variety and articulation in various styles can only be fully accomplished by careful and active listening.

The following articulation markings are commonly used by arrangers to produce specific effects and are necessary for the players or singers to know exactly how to perform a given passage. The arranger must use these markings, especially if there is more than one possible interpretation of a passage. In other words, the arranger must show *exactly* how each part should be articulated, leaving nothing to chance:

TYPE   *HOW PERFORMED*

Caps      The quarter notes are accented forcefully and shortened.

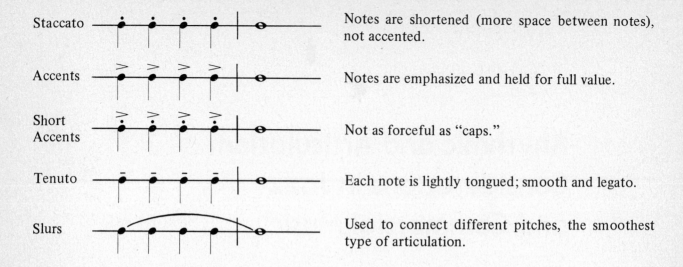

Staccato		Notes are shortened (more space between notes), not accented.
Accents		Notes are emphasized and held for full value.
Short Accents		Not as forceful as "caps."
Tenuto		Each note is lightly tongued; smooth and legato.
Slurs		Used to connect different pitches, the smoothest type of articulation.

Familiarize yourself with the markings given; listen for what each articulation will produce when saxophones or brass use them in various rhythmic contexts. Each type of articulation produces slightly different results depending on note types and tempos; so it is important to "sing" your lines and articulate them accordingly.

Following are some rhythmic principles that are used in jazz and other styles of commercial music. These principles should be regarded only as generalities, however, because of the many variables afforded by style, tempo, meter, orchestration, and so forth.

1. An anticipation is accented if tied over or added to a longer note value:

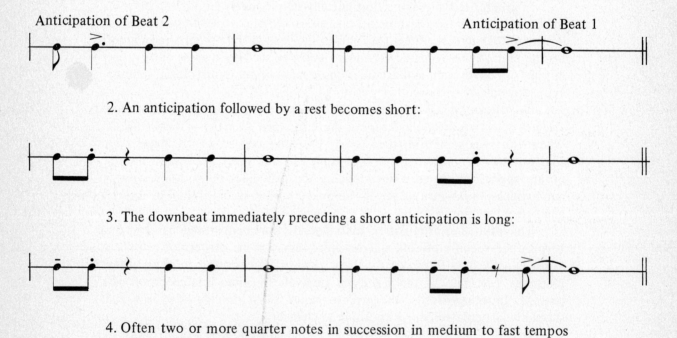

2. An anticipation followed by a rest becomes short:

3. The downbeat immediately preceding a short anticipation is long:

4. Often two or more quarter notes in succession in medium to fast tempos will be short and separated:

72

5. In slow to medium tempos, however, successive quarter notes can be long and connected (but not always):

In all tempos be sure to articulate successive quarter notes wherever ambiguities might exist.

6. Avoid inconsistencies as follows:

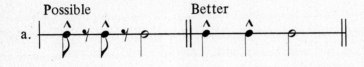

a.

Each example will sound the same, but the second is easier to read.

b.

The difference here is very slight, but the second example is preferred.

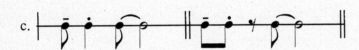

c.

Although the first version is often used, the second is preferred.

Avoid ties where they are not really played as ties:

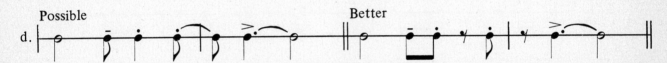

7. If the arrangement is in swing style, write "Swing" at the beginning of each part. Eighth notes will then be interpreted as follows:

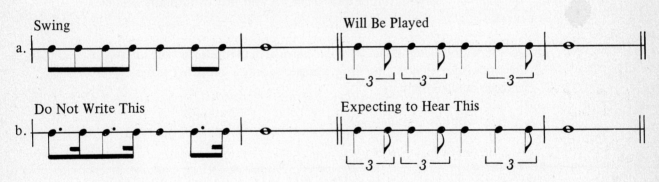

If you want rock or Latin-style even eighth notes, write "Even Eighths" or "Rock" or "Latin" at the top of each part so that there is no confusion as to style of eighth notes.

8. In styles where the eighth notes are interpreted as part of triplets, the downbeat is rarely short with the immediate upbeat long:

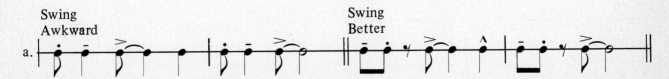

In styles with even eighth notes, downbeats and upbeats work well both long and short:

Even 8ths

The most important guideline here is the following: does the line sound right in the desired style and tempo when played or sung?

9. Try for a blend of

1. Downbeats
2. Anticipations
3. Rests
4. Longer note values

Write what sounds good within a given style, unified but not redundant, "hip" but not affected, elegant but not ornate.

This quickly becomes too predictable:

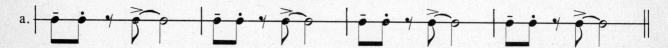

This is simply too cluttered:

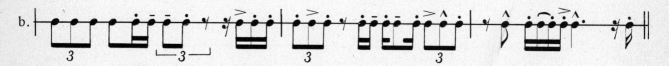

Many melodies contain built-in rhythmic repetitions. This is good, for repetitions make for unity if not carried to an extreme. But there is often a fine dividing line between unity and absurdity; do not overdo any one idea or device.

10. Do not overburden the line with excessive articulations; rather, emphasize the important points, marking phrase endings, accented notes, legato passages, and so forth.

This phrase, without articulations

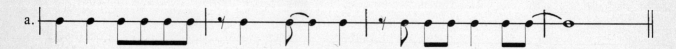

may be interpreted any number of ways including the two versions shown now:

Even 8ths

Swing

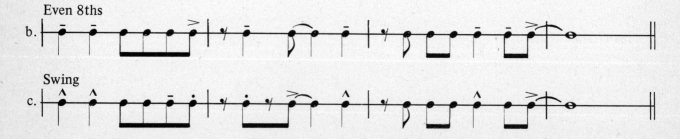

Example C would be close to what many jazz-oriented musicians would play if left to their own instincts; however, to be on the safe side, particularly when dealing with less experienced players and to ensure that experienced players interpret a passage the way you want them to on first reading, be explicit in the important areas.

CLASS EXERCISES

Articulate the following fragments in the indicated styles and tempos.

1. Lightly Swinging, Moderate Tempo

2. Medium Slow Ballad

3. Fast Jazz Waltz

4. Moderate Swing

5. Medium Bossa Nova

6. Very Slow Swing

7. Medium Country Rock

Assignment: Do Worksheets 39 and 40.

22

Rhythmic Variation

Following is a five-note phrase that will be varied using combinations of rhythmic anticipations and rests:

Original

Sing each variation three times (in fast, medium, and slow tempos) in swing style and three times (fast, medium, and slow) with even eighth notes. Keep in mind the principles of articulation and note how each fragment could be interpreted using different combinations of articulations.

Variations with one rhythmic anticipation:

Variations with two anticipations:

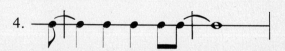

5.

6.

7.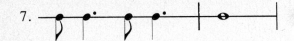

8.

9.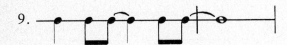

10.

Variations with three anticipations:

1.

2.

3.

4.

5.

6.

7.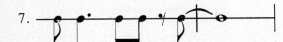

8.

9.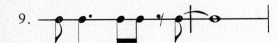

10.

Variations with four anticipations:

1.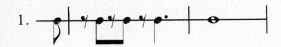

2.

3.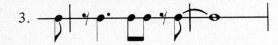

4.

5.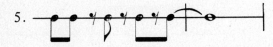

One variation with five anticipations:

1.

Five-note patterns starting with a quarter rest:

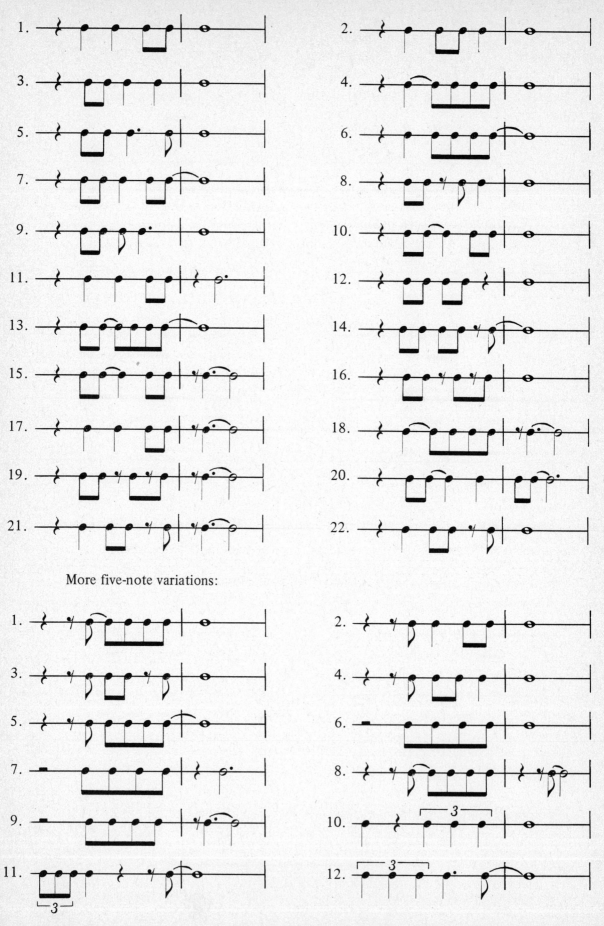

More five-note variations:

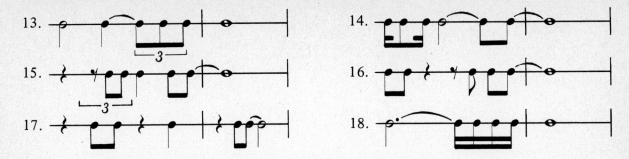

You have just been given seventy-one variants on a five-note motive; these are just some of the possibilities using only five notes. Not all the foregoing rhythmic patterns will fit all five-note motives, however, so make intelligent choices from the examples, or compose your own variations to set a given melodic contour.

CLASS EXERCISES

Following are fragments from standard tunes. Set each of these four different ways according to the principles given. Using various tempos, fast, medium, and slow, you will quickly discover which rhythms sound natural and unforced while others may not sound right at any tempo. As you can see, rhythmic variation is almost limitless; so use your imagination to compose your own variations. Label each example with a tempo and style marking.

3.

3.a

3.b

3.c

3.d

4.

4.a

4.b

4.c

4.d

Assignment: Do Worksheets 41 and 42.

23

Melodic Embellishment: The Passing Tone

We have seen that leadsheet rhythms tend to be simplistic and often rather "square." Altering these rhythms is an important aspect of the arranger's craft to make an often pedestrian melody "swing." The addition of new tones—tones that do not occur in the original—is the next area we must explore. Melodic changes can be thought of as being embellishments of the melody that fall into three categories: passing tones, neighboring tones, and other chord members.

The first of these embellishment techniques, the passing tone, involves the filling in of intervals by stepwise motion either diatonically or chromatically or by a combination of the two. Notice also how rhythmic variation is used.

Original

EXAMPLE 1.

Embellished:

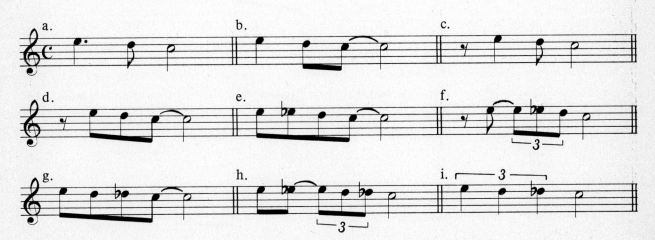

Original:

EXAMPLE 2.

Embellished:

Original:

EXAMPLE 3.

Embellished:

Obviously, not all the possible diatonic and chromatic passing tone variations work in all situations. Attention must be paid to harmonic implications, style, tempo, instrumentation, and dynamic level in working out passsing tone embellishments.

Notice how melodic tones were occasionally repeated in the examples given. This repeating technique is often desirable to use in conjunction with any of the other devices for melodic variation.

CLASS EXERCISES

Vary the following fragments using both diatonic and chromatic passing tones and rhythmic variation:

a.

b.

c.

d.

e.

f.

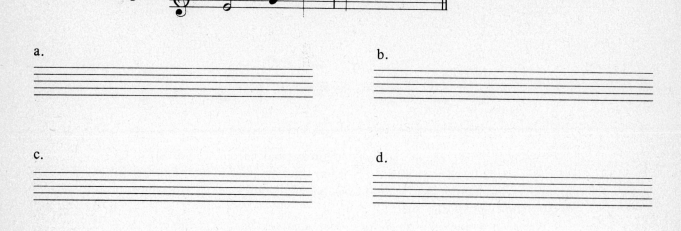

Original — Ami7 — D7

a.

b.

c.

d.

e.

f.

Assignment: Do Worksheets 43 and 44.

24

Melodic Embellishment: The Neighboring Tone

A neighboring tone, by definition, is a tone that lies a half step or whole step on either side of a given note. Neighboring tones can be used melodically either in an accented or unaccented form, that is, on strong or weak beats or parts of beats. Study the following examples of the many uses of neighboring tones; notice that neighboring tones must resolve to a normal melody note and are never left by leap.

EXAMPLE 1. Diatonic neighboring tones, both unaccented and accented:

Original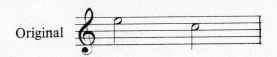

Unaccented variants:

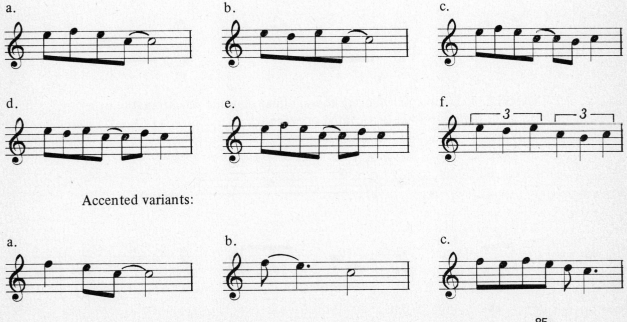

Accented variants:

EXAMPLE 2. Chromatic neighboring tones, unaccented and accented:

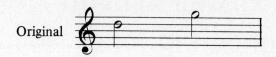

Original

Unaccented variants:

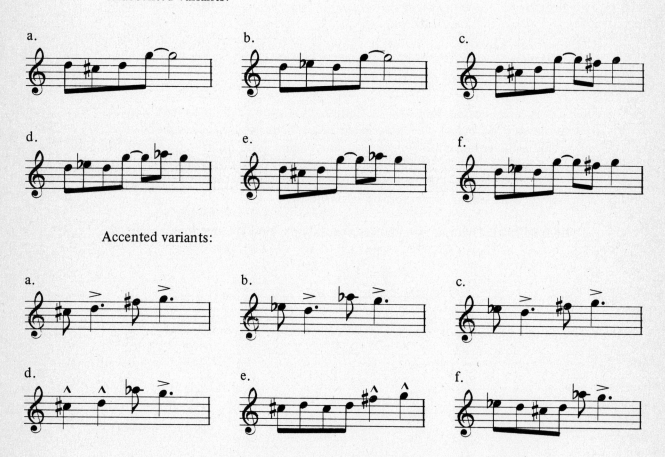

a.

b.

c.

d.

e.

f.

Accented variants:

a.

b.

c.

d.

e.

f.

EXAMPLE 3. Double neighboring tones, either diatonic or chromatic, or a mixture of the two, either unaccented or accented:

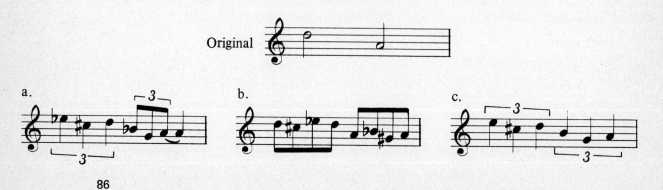

Original

a.

b.

c.

Chromatic neighboring tones, either single or double, must be handled with a great deal of caution as not all possibilities will "work" in all instances. Choices must be made keeping in mind the basic melodic contour and, above all, the harmonic implications.

Let us explore the harmonic treatment of some of the double neighboring tone passages illustrated by setting them in four-part block. For instance, Examples 3a and 3b work quite well harmonized as follows:

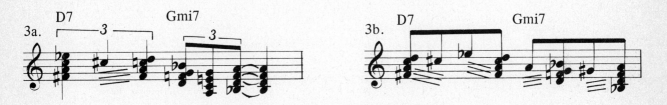

Remember that the angled dashes are a kind of "musical shorthand" signifying the half-step shift. If necessary, review the chapters on harmonizing nonchordal tones.

CLASS EXERCISES

Vary the following fragments using as many of the following techniques as possible within the bounds of good taste:

1. Rhythmic changes and articulations
2. Passing tones
3. Single diatonic neighboring tones, above and below
4. Double diatonic neighboring tones
5. Single chromatic neighboring tones, above and below
6. Double chromatic neighboring tones

Observe the harmonic structure; harmonize the following in four-part open or closed block.

Assignment: Do Worksheets 45 and 46.

25

Melodic Embellishment: Other Chord Tones

In addition to the rhythmic and melodic devices that we have covered so far, we may use other chord members to vary a given melody:

If we use passing tones, neighboring tones, other chord members, and rhythmic devices, we find that we now have virtually all the techniques necessary to vary a melody in any style:

CLASS EXERCISES

Vary the following fragments using other chord members, passing and neighboring tones, and rhythmic devices.

Assignment: Use Worksheet 47 to write a melodic arrangement of BILL BAILEY.

26

The Rhythm Section:
Bass Lines

Two instruments currently used as rhythm bass instruments in all types of commercial music are the acoustic and electric basses. Rock-oriented groups usually use a bass guitar and jazz-oriented groups often use the string bass. For the purposes of this study, we are concerned only with the linear considerations that apply equally well to either type of bass instrument since the stringing, tuning, and notation of each are the same. Hereafter we simply refer to "bass" without distinction as to type.

The four strings of the bass are notated as follows:

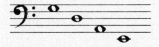

Keep in mind, however, that the actual sound is an octave lower than notated.

In swing and most jazz styles, the most common bass part is what is known as a "walking" bass line. This type of line is generally a steady pulse of quarter notes, with occasional eighth notes and triplets for variety.

Experienced bass players often prefer to have a part consisting of the chord symbols alone, which allows them to create their own lines. In ensemble situations, however, a written bass part with chord symbols assures that desired effects such as contrary motion with the melody, anticipations, octave-tutti passages, specific inversions, and so forth are achieved. A written-out bass part is necessary, therefore, to guarantee that the arrangement is played as desired by the arranger. A bass part with chord symbols and the instructions "Walk" or "Ad Lib" allows experienced players to create their own part.

The following guidelines are helpful in constructing sensible bass lines.

1. Write the root on the first beat of the chord change (exceptions are noted later):

2. Use diatonic or chromatic passing tones or other chord tones on weak beats (beats other than one):

3. Approach new chords by step from above or below—or from previous root:

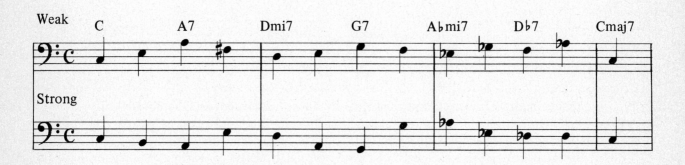

4. Avoid "pattern" lines such as the old boogie-woogie line (R-3-5-6-8) unless this rather dated line is desired:

5. Do not use strictly arpeggiated lines; stepwise motion with occasional arpeggios is smoother:

6. Try for contrary motion with the melody; always avoid parallel octaves between the melody and bass line (unless used in octave-tutti passages):

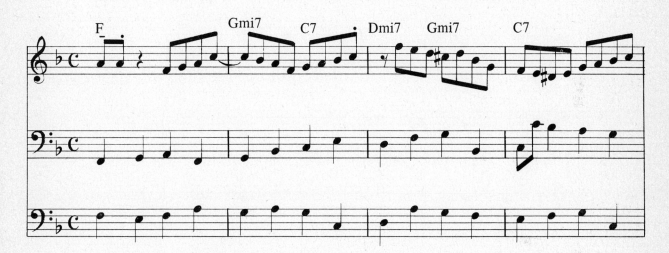

Which of the bass lines shown is more satisfactory? Can you spot all the errors in the weaker version? Remember that, if you leave the construction of the bass line to the bass player by providing chord symbols only, errors in voice leading and coupling are bound to occur.

7. The bass line (as well as the entire rhythm section) should not catch all the anticipations in the melody. Some anticipations, however, particularly the heavily accented ones, may be written into the bass line. (This is the exception to the rule that all voices anticipate with the melody.):

Sometimes the bass part as well as the entire rhythm section can have the important rhythms of the leadline as in the example shown in the first two measures. This is very effective for accents, sudden changes in the usual rhythmic flow, and momentary extra emphasis; do not overuse this technique, however, because it can lead to a choppy effect.

Following are a number of "stock" lines based on the II-V-I progression. Note how chromatic tones are handled—always as passing tones.

Two-beat patterns:

Bass lines for turnaround progression:

Here is a bass part for a simple rock progression in the key of F:

Here is a bass line for a blues progression in the key of C:

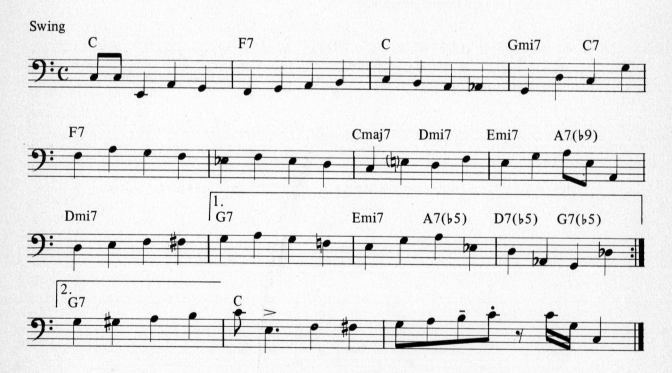

Study the examples, noticing how the first sets up a rhythmic pattern as well as covering the roots. The second example is more linear and gives a good solid feeling for swing style.

CLASS EXERCISES

Provide bass lines for the following:

Assignment: Use Worksheet 48 to write a bass part for your arrangment of BILL BAILEY.

27

The Rhythm Section: Piano and Guitar

In many commercial music and jazz situations, the piano and guitar parts are often only "road maps" for the player, providing chord symbols, rests, and essential rhythms. The players create their own part in performance, interpreting the symbols in various voicings and rhythms appropriate to the style of the arrangement. Piano and guitar parts are therefore often rather sparse in format, leaving much to the background and instincts of the player.

On the other hand, a piano part can be a two-staff part completely written out, with all voicings and rhythms notated exactly as to be played. Guitar parts may also be written this way in one staff, but because this requires a complete knowledge of the instrument and its technique, a fully notated guitar part is often unnecessary and simply too much work for the arranger.

If an arrangement requires specific voicings for the piano or guitar, they may be notated with chord symbols to facilitate reading:

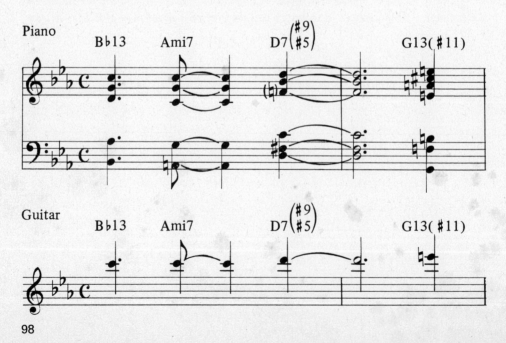

In situations such as that just given, when writing guitar parts, it is better to show only the top voice, allowing the player to voice the chord in the most convenient way. (Remember that the guitar sounds an octave lower than is notated.)

When there are no special rhythms or voicings indicated, piano and guitar parts can simply consist of chord symbols with slashes to signify beats. The slashes are not quarter notes per se unless a steady quarter note rhythm is desired and specifically indicated (as in a Basie guitar part):

Specific rhythms are indicated by stemmed and beamed slashes and diamond-shaped notes with chord symbols above them:

Piano or Guitar

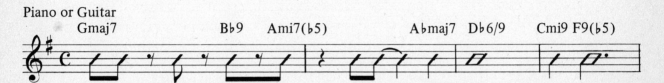

This kind of part should be written only if a very special result is desired. Do not try to catch all the anticipations and intricate rhythms that the brass or saxophones are playing, because this will impede the even rhythmic flow of the arrangement.

A piano or guitar part can include both types of slashes as well as standard notation:

Piano or Guitar

Aside from chord symbols, a guitar part may consist of single line passages:

Guitar (w/saxs)

Two-part writing for the guitar—thirds, fourths, fifths, sixths, sevenths, and octaves—are relatively easy to play, but seconds can be awkward and should usually be avoided:

Guitar

Anything more than that shown requires a specialized knowledge of the instrument and should not be attempted without further study of the guitar and its technique.

CLASS EXERCISES

Write a practical piano or guitar part for the following fragments. Use the several varieties of notation discussed in the text.

Assignment: Do Worksheet 49.

28

The Rhythm Section: Additional Considerations in Writing Piano, Bass, and Guitar Parts

In the following passage

EXAMPLE 1.

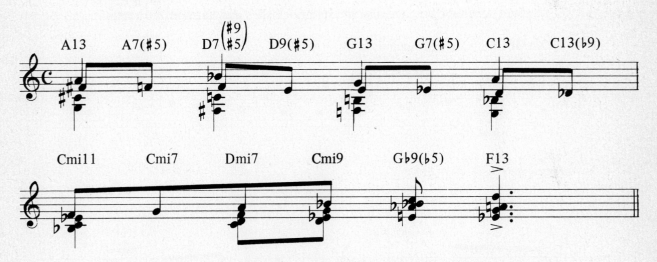

the rate of harmonic change is very fast, with a change of harmony every half beat until the last chord. It would be absurd to have the piano and guitar try to catch every alteration as it occurs, particularly if the tempo is medium to fast. Even if this were very slow, it would not be desirable for the guitar to be "chung-chunging" on every eighth note. A compromise must be reached, therefore, by deciding what the principal chord "feel" is and simplifying the symbols to what will best render the harmonic "feel."

This will meet our needs for the passage quite well:

In the first measure we have indicated the chord on the downbeats, leaving the chromatic alterations as unaccented variants of the chords we are notating. In the second measure, Cmi7 serves for both forms of the chord—Cmi11 and Cmi9. The Dmi7 chord is really a passing structure (even though it is accented) and need not be indicated.

Accented alterations of the fifth should be added to the chord symbol, but alterations of the ninth need not be; a simple seventh chord is all that need be written. For example, this

Rather than

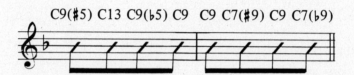

Study the following melody and its embellished and harmonized version:

EXAMPLE 2. Original version:

EXAMPLE 2a. Embellished and harmonized version:

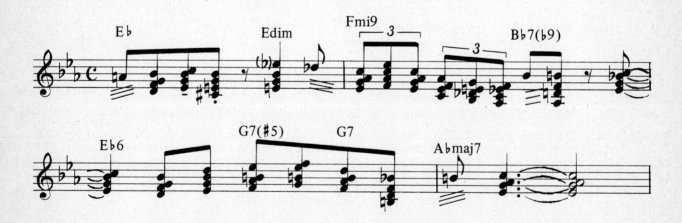

Analyze Example 2a, noting how the basic melody can still be found among the added passing, neighboring, and additional chord tones.

Following is the literal harmonic and rhythmic representation of Example 2a:

EXAMPLE 2b.

Dmaj9 Ebmaj9 Eb6 Edim   Edim(addEb) Gbmi9 Fmi9 Fmi7 Fmi9 Fmi7 Gdim Fmi7

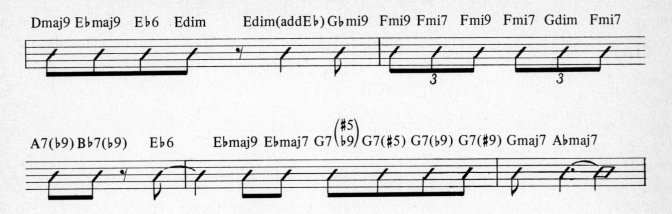

A7(b9) Bb7(b9)   Eb6   Ebmaj9 Ebmaj7 G7(#5/b9) G7(#5) G7(b9) G7(#9) Gmaj7 Abmaj7

Example 2b is a good illustration of what *not* to write for a normal piano or guitar part; it is far too complex.

Accented neighboring chords such as:

can be represented in the rhythm section parts as:

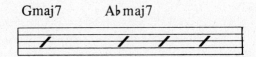

The main melody note C is thought of as an anticipation to beat two; the neighboring chord harmonizes beat one.

The following rhythm part for Example 1 illustrates the principles of simplified chord structures and accented neighboring chords:

EXAMPLE 2c.

Dmaj9 Ebmaj9 Edim   Fmi9   A7(b9) Bb7(b9) Eb   G7(#5) G7 Gmaj7 Abmaj7

In fast to very fast tempos, streamline the rhythm parts for a smooth effect, as in Example 2d:

EXAMPLE 2d.

Eb   Edim   Fmi9   Bb7(b9)   Eb   G7   Abmaj7

The bass part may be simplified even more than in the previous example (2d). Omit the chord extensions, alterations and the half-step shift chords, leaving only the main chord symbols:

EXAMPLE 2e.

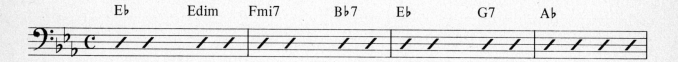

Examples 2b–2e show the process of simplification needed for writing good rhythm parts. While the part may consist of basic chord symbols only, remember that, if you want concerted motion in the rhythm section, each part may be so indicated. Example 2f illustrates yet another possible rhythm part for Example 2a:

EXAMPLE 2f.

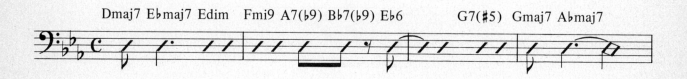

CLASS EXERCISES

Write rhythm parts for the following melodic fragments. Simplify, using your best judgment.

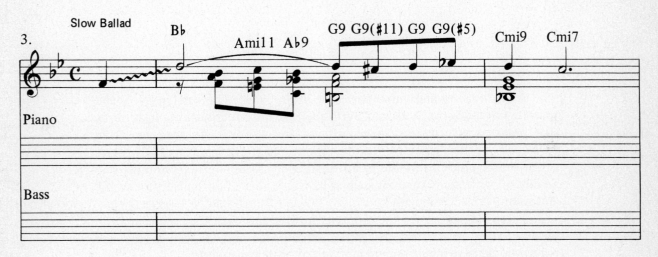

Assignment: Do Worksheets 50 and 51; use Worksheet 52 to write a piano/guitar part for your arrangement of BILL BAILEY.

29

The Rhythm Section: Percussion Parts

As with piano and guitar parts, the drum part can be written freely and sparsely, notating only crucial parts such as introductions, endings, rests, solo breaks, tutti rhythms, special effects, and so forth. An adequate drum part need only be a guide for the player, since what a drummer actually plays is far too complex to notate in a realistic part. Drummers, then, must rely mainly on written instructions such as half-time rock, slow ballad, fast swing, and so on.

These indications tell the drummer how to approach the arrangement in terms of style. In addition to a style marking, the part (as well as all of the parts) should have a metronome marking of beats per minute.

Drum parts may consist of standard notational conventions as well as slashes to indicate beats (not quarter notes). A style and tempo marking, dynamic marking, and special instructions, if any, along with the word "play" tells the drummer to lay down a standard beat, free to add whatever will enhance the arrangement with his or her improvisational skill.

Following are some sample fragments of drum parts:

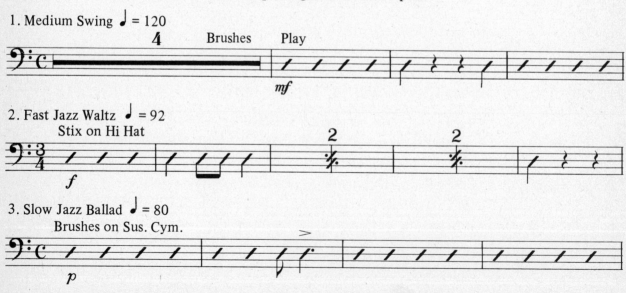

To indicate specific instruments, such as cymbals, bass drum, and cow bell, different areas of the staff are used along with an abbreviation of the name of the instrument. The following or any other adequate abbreviations may be used in drum parts. Uncommon instruments as well as nonstandard ways of playing standard instruments should be indicated in written-out form.

The following are just a few of the instruments and techniques that a drummer can be instructed to play. Use additional drum books as resources for other possible percussion instruments and techniques.

Snare drum	S.D.	Cymbal	Cym.
Bass drum	B.D.	Triangle	Tri.
Tom tom(s)	T.T.(s)	Wood block	W.B.
High hat	H.H.	Tambourine	Tamb.
Closed high hat	Cl. H.H.	Cowbell	C.B.

On dome of cymbal	Gong (or tam tam)
Sizzle cymbal	Snares off
Bass drum with tympani mallets	Snares on
Floor tom with soft mallets	Rim shot
Bell tree	Jingle ring
Ratchet	On rims
Bird whistle	Maracas
Police whistle	Guiro
Slide whistle	Claves
Temple blocks	Castanets

In addition to the use of slashes, drums can be represented by noteheads and cymbals by "X's" with stems and beams:

Different sizes of tom toms are represented in various space areas of the staff to indicate relative pitch:

The triangle and high hat are two instruments that may be played either open (o) or closed (+).

Any arrangement in a special style of jazz, rock, Latin, disco, or any other type that could have various interpretations when dealing with a style marking only should include the basic beat or pattern for the drummer. With the basic beat pattern notated, the drummer is expected to use this as a guide only, adding to the basic beat in good taste according to his or her musical abilities.

The following are basic patterns a drummer may see in a part:

1. Medium Rock

2. Jazz Rock

3. Rock Shuffle

4. Disco

There are, or course, a large number of possible patterns in the many styles of commercial music. It is not within the scope of this method to give a complete table of these, so it would be of value to the arranger to have a book written for drummers showing additional patterns and notational conventions.

Following is a list of notational devices that should be understood fully:

1. A single slash through the stem of a note divides it into eighth notes; two slashes divides it into sixteenth notes; three slashes converts it to an unmeasured roll:

Each of these represents unmeasured rolls of various durations on cymbals or drums.

2. This is a single-measure repeat. These can be strung together but should not be continued on to another line. Note how measures are numbered.

3. This is a two-measure repeat. There are *no* acceptable symbols for repeats longer than two measures other than:

In other words, this is not acceptable:

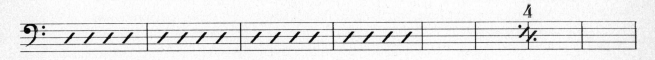

4. Fills can be notated this way:

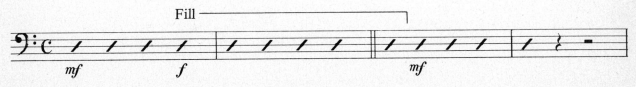

5. Ensemble rhythms can be cued in the drum part this way:

6. To indicate specific rhythms in the drum part, use slashes with stems. This tells the drummer to play the notated rhythm only, using any appropriate combination of drums and cymbals:

7. When no specific rhythms are required, that is, when all that is needed is for the drummer to simply play rhythm, large sections may be written out as follows:

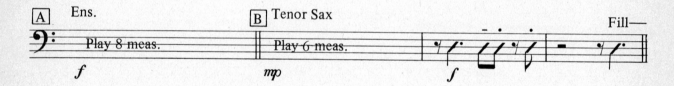

When using this sectional type of notation, it is wise to indicate what is happening by writing "Saxs," "Trom solo," "Ens.," and so on, as a helpful device for the drummer to keep his or her place in the arrangement and to best complement each section.

CLASS EXERCISES

Analyze the following demonstration arrangement of BILLY BOY found on pages 111-118 of the text. Study the rhythm section parts to see how they are arranged to complement the ensemble.

Assignment: Use Worksheet 53 to write a drum part for your arrangement of BILL BAILEY. Use commercially available manuscript paper to transpose and copy the ensemble parts from your score, and, using the rhythm section parts already completed, play your arrangement of BILL BAILEY and the demonstration arrangement BILLY BOY. (The parts for BILLY BOY are found on pages 120-126 of the text.)

After playing BILL BAILEY, use Worksheet 54 to arrange the standard tune PENNIES FROM HEAVEN.

30

"Billy Boy":
Demonstration Arrangement

Following is a jazz-flavored arrangement of BILLY BOY scored for trumpet, two saxophones, trombone, and rhythm section. The original version of this folk song is included for comparison with the embellished version.

BILLY BOY

113

114

At this point there is a melodic extension that serves as a coda.

117

31

"Billy Boy": Parts

Bb Trumpet

Medium Swing Tempo ♩ = 112-120

Eb Alto Saxophone

Medium Swing Tempo ♩ = 112-120

B♭ Tenor Saxophone

Medium Swing Tempo ♩ = 112-120

Trombone

BILLY BOY

Bass

Medium Swing Tempo ♩ = 112-120

BILLY BOY

Drums

Medium Swing Tempo ♩ = 112-120

32

Melodic and Rhythmic Creative Sections: Introductions

Creative sections in an arrangement are those areas in which the melody or tune is not present, is fragmented, or is momentarily static such as in endings, introductions, and turnarounds. The next few chapters explore these creative sections where the melodic line is freely composed or improvised, not necessarily following or embellishing a preset melody.

In all cases we have furnished the chords or harmonic foundation for these creative sections, since harmonic progression is an element not yet introduced in this series.

The first section we will explore is introductions. In general, an introduction uses contrasting orchestration to set up the first statement of the melody, but this varies from style to style depending upon the purpose of the arrangement. Some arrangements may use no introduction at all, others may incorporate part of the tune for introductory material, and still others may have an introduction that seems to have no relationship whatsoever to the forthcoming music. The strongest introduction, then, depends upon the purpose of the arrangement (is it for dancing, easy listening, entertainment?) and the effect wanted from an introduction.

Following are several techniques for composing an introduction. These techniques are not all the possible variations, but they are some of the more useful and practical when dealing with a four-part ensemble with rhythm section and when limited to four-part open- or closed-block voicing.

1. Use rhythm section only; the piano plays ad lib throughout the introduction in the indicated style:

Medium Swing—Solo Intro
Piano

2. A solo instrument (including piano and guitar) plays a composed melody based on the chords of the introduction; rhythm section also plays:

3. A combination of instruments plays a unison or octave melody line. This works well for saxs:

4. The complete ensemble plays a harmonized rhythmic introduction, using punches, repeated notes, and so forth:

CLASS EXERCISES

Compose introductions for the following as indicated.

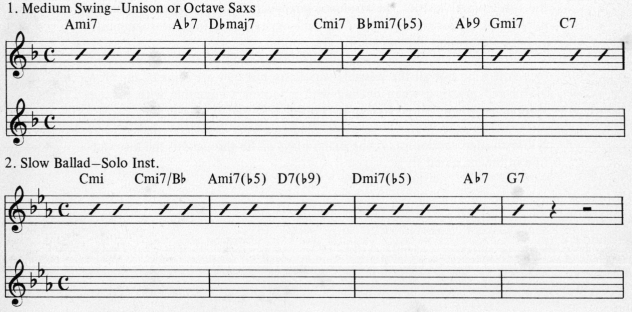

1. Medium Swing—Unison or Octave Saxs

2. Slow Ballad—Solo Inst.

Assignment: Do Worksheets 55 and 56.

128

33

Melodic and Rhythmic Creative Sections: Fills

Fills are used to maintain interest and to continue the established motion when the melody reaches points of repose. These points occur in various places in the course of a tune, for instance, at the end of each section of an A-A-B-A form, as well as within phrases. Fills often function as introductions for the next phrase.

Fills can be played by the lead instrument or section, or by accompanying instruments while the lead instrument or section sustains or drops out. Fills can be solos, single lines, duets, or fully harmonized melodies played by the entire ensemble.

The important thing for a fill is that it be organic. That is, it must "grow" out of what has happened immediately before and lead into what happens next. They must make musical sense and sound natural, flowing, and unforced. Write fills that are in the style of the arrangement—not something just "put in" to fill up space.

Analyze the following melodic fragment and the various ways of filling the static seven beats:

1. Written out solo alto sax fill:

2. Ad lib solo alto sax fill (the chord changes are in concert pitch):

3. Written out solo fill for piano:

4. Ad lib solo fill for piano:

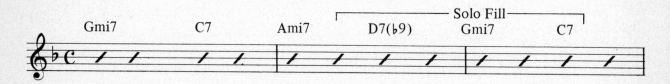

5. Written solo break for bass:

6. Ad lib solo break for bass:

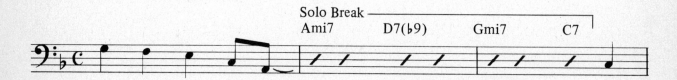

7. Written solo break for drums:

8. Ad lib solo break for drums:

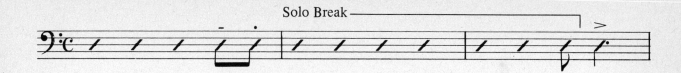

Solo Break

9. Two or more instruments play a unison or octave line:

10. Entire ensemble plays a composed fill harmonized in block:

11. Melody sustains with independent inner voice motion:

12. The entire ensemble plays rhythmic punches, repeated notes. The rhythm sustains the interest:

Following is an analysis of the fills used in the arrangement of BILLY BOY found on pages 111-118 of the text. Study each example, noting how the prinicples given for writing fills have been used in each case.

1. Measures 7, 8 and 29–32: two saxs play a unison fill.
2. Measure 8: drum fill.
3. Measure 15: solo trumpet pick-up to modulation.
4. Measures 23, 24: ensemble fill.
5. Measure 34: tutti octave fill.
6. Measure 38: bass solo fill.

The foregoing examples are just some of the ways in which each situation could be handled. Note also how the rhythm section is used in each instance.

CLASS EXERCISES

Compose fills suitable for each instance indicated. Harmonize and embellish the original version and indicate exactly who plays each fill. Include style and tempo markings.

4.

Assignment: Do Worksheets 57 and 58.

34

Melodic and Rhythmic Creative Sections: Endings

Endings are extensions, abrupt surprises, or other ways of establishing a feeling of finality. For now, since all chord progressions are given and the measure sequences are set, use only the following techniques for writing endings.

1. The entire ensemble continues in full block, up to the final note:

2. The final note may come after a strong finish or after a subdued "wind-down" sequence:

3. A ballad may ritard to a fermata:

4. The last note may be several places rhythmically:

5. The ending may be rhythmic with repeated notes—perhaps similar to material used in the introduction:

CLASS EXERCISES

Compose endings based on the chord progression given. Add dynamics, style and tempo markings.

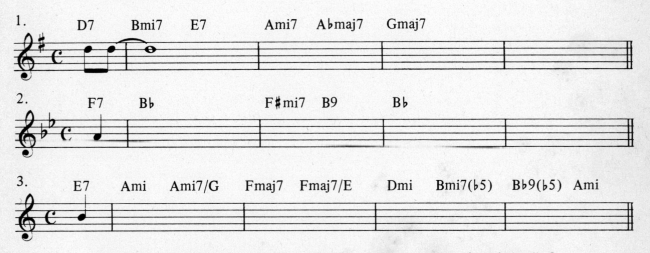

Assignment: Do Worksheets 59, 60, and 61. Choose several leadsheets from Appendix 2 and arrange on additional score paper, using all or any of the various techniques of open- and closed-block voicing, chord choices, inner voice motion, rhythmic and melodic embellishment, rhythm section writing, and composing introductions, fills, and endings. Include style and tempo markings; copy parts and play.

WORKSHEET 1

Date _____   Name _____

The following chords are in root position; label each with the correct symbol.

1.   2.   3.   4.

5.   6.   7.   8.

9.   10.   11.   12.

13.   14.   15.   16.

17.   18.   19.   20.

21.   22.   23.   24.

WORKSHEET 2

Date _____   Name _____

The following chords are in first inversion; label each with the correct symbol.

WORKSHEET 3

Date _____   Name _____

Write four-note chords in root position as indicated by the following symbols.

1. G♭mi7   2. A♭maj7   3. F♯mi7(♭5)   4. D♭mi(maj7)

5. G6   6. E7   7. E♭dim   8. Emi6

9. B7(♭5)   10. Amaj7(♯5)   11. D7(♯5)   12. B♭maj7(♭5)

13. A♭dim   14. G♭6   15. C♯mi7   16. E♭mi(maj7)

17. F♯mi6   18. C♭7   19. Dmi7(♭5)   20. Dmaj7

21. F7(♯5)   22. Amaj7   23. C♯7(♭5)   24. Emaj7

WORKSHEET 4

Date _____   Name _____

Write four-note chords in first inversion as indicated by the following symbols.

1. G♭maj7   2. A♭mi7(♭5)   3. F♯mi(maj7)   4. D♭6

5. G7   6. Edim   7. E♭mi6   8. E7(♭5)

9. Bmaj7(♯5)   10. A7(♯5)   11. Dmaj7(♭5)   12. B♭dim

13. A♭6   14. Fmi7   15. C♯mi(maj7)   16. E♭mi6

17. F♯7   18. C♭mi7(♭5)   19. Dmaj7(♭5)   20. B♭7(♯5)

21. Fmaj7   22. A7(♭5)   23. C♯maj7(♯5)   24. Emi7

Date _____   Name _____

Write four-part closed-block voicings for the following chords using R, 3, 5, and either 6
or 7 for melody notes. Use accidentals for all voicings rather than key signatures. For a
simple symbol without either a sixth or major seventh indicated, voice both the sixth and
major seventh melody notes.

1.   A

2.   Cmi

3.   Eb6

4.   Gb

5.   Bbmaj7

6.   Dbmi

7.   Emi6

8.   Gmi

9.   Bmi(maj7)

10. D

11. Fmaj7

12. Abmi(maj7)

WORKSHEET 6

Date _____   Name _____

Write four-part closed-block voicings for the following chords. Follow the instructions given for Worksheet 5.

1. F#6

2. Bmaj7

3. Dmi

4. E♭

5. G

6. Bmi

7. `Cmi6

8. Emi(maj7)

9. A♭maj7

10. Ami

11. C#mi(maj7)

12. F

When finished, check your work twice to make sure that there are no half steps between the top two voices.

142

Date _____   Name _____

Write four-part closed-block voicings for the following chords using R, 3, 5, and 7 for melody notes. Use accidentals for all voicings rather than key signatures.

1. C7

2. Dmi7

3. C#dim

4. Emi

5. Eb7

6. D7

7. Abdim

8. Abmi7

9. F#7

10. Bdim

11. Gdim

12. Dbmi7

When finished, check your work twice to make sure that there are no half steps between the top two voices.

Date _____   Name _____

Write four-part closed-block voicings for the following chords. Follow the instructions given for Worksheet 7.

1. B7(♭5)   2. Fmi7(♭5)

3. D7(♯5)   4. G♭mi7(♭5)

5. C♯mi7(♭5)   6. E7(♯5)

7. F♯7(♯5)   8. A7(♭5)

9. D♭mi7(♭5)   10. B♭7(♭5)

11. C7(♭5)   12. G7(♯5)

Date _____   Name _____

The following chords are in root position; label each with the correct symbol.

WORKSHEET 10

Date _____   Name _____

Write five-note chords in root position as indicated by the following symbols.

1. G7(♯9)   2. B♭maj9   3. D♭7(♭9)   4. Fmi(maj9)

5. E7$\left(\begin{smallmatrix}♭9\\♭5\end{smallmatrix}\right)$ 6. A♭mi9   7. B7$\left(\begin{smallmatrix}♯9\\♯5\end{smallmatrix}\right)$ 8. Dmi9(♭5)

9. F♯7$\left(\begin{smallmatrix}♭9\\♯5\end{smallmatrix}\right)$ 10. E♭9   11. A7$\left(\begin{smallmatrix}♯9\\♭5\end{smallmatrix}\right)$ 12. C9(♭5)

13. B♭6/9   14. G♭9(♯5)   15. Gmi6/9   16. Amaj9

17. Bmi(maj9)   18. A♭7$\left(\begin{smallmatrix}♭9\\♭5\end{smallmatrix}\right)$ 19. C♯mi9   20. D7$\left(\begin{smallmatrix}♭9\\♯5\end{smallmatrix}\right)$

21. D♭9(♭5)   22. E9   23. C♭6/9   24. Fmi9

146

WORKSHEET 11

Date _____   Name _____

Write four-part closed-block voicings for the following ninth chords, the melody notes
being R, 9, 3, 5, and 6 or 7. Use only the sixth in 6/9 chords; all others will use the seventh. Use accidentals in all voicings.

1. Dmaj9

2. Fmi9

3. G♭9

4. Bmi(maj9)

5. Bmi9

6. A♭6/9

7. Gmaj9

8. E♭mi6/9

9. E♭9

10. Emi(maj9)

11. C♯6/9

12. Ami6/9

147

Date _____   Name _____

Write four-part closed-block voicings following the instructions given for Worksheet 11.

1. Ebmi9   2.   A6/9

3. Emi9   4.   Bb9

5. Abmaj9   6.   Dmi6/9

7. C9   8.   F6/9

9. Bbmi(maj9)   10. Dbmaj9

11. F#mi6/9   12. Gbmi(maj9)

WORKSHEET 13

Date _____   Name _____

Write four-part closed-block voicings using the melody notes R, 3, 7, and the appropriate ninth and fifth. Use accidentals in all voicings.

1. Dmi9(♭5)

2. G♭7(♭9/♭5)

3. D♭7(♭9)

4. G9(♭5)

5. A9(♯5)

6. D7(♯9)

7. B7(♭9/♯5)

8. Emi9(♭5)

9. A♭9(♭5)

10. E♭9(♯5)

11. B♭mi9(♭5)

12. F7(♯9/♯5)

149

WORKSHEET 14

Date _____   Name _____

Write four-part closed-block voicings for the following chords using the melody notes R, 3, 7, and the appropriate ninth and fifth. Use accidentals in all voicings.

1. Eb7(b9)

2. G9(#5)

3. Bb7($\begin{smallmatrix}\#9\\b5\end{smallmatrix}$)

4. Gb7($\begin{smallmatrix}b9\\b5\end{smallmatrix}$)

5. Dbmi(maj7)

6. Emi9

7. A7($\begin{smallmatrix}b9\\\#5\end{smallmatrix}$)

8. Bmi9(b5)

9. Ab7(#9)

10. Dmi9

11. F9

12. C9(b5)

150

WORKSHEET 15

Date _____   Name _____

Write four-part closed-block voicings for the following chords using all available melody notes. Use accidentals in all voicings.

1. Db6/9

2. A9(b5)

3. Dmi(maj7)

4. F#7(#5)

5. Abmi7(b5)

6. Fmaj9

7. Edim

8. Bbmi9

9. Cmi7

10. Gmi6

11. Bbmi6/9

12. Ebmi(maj9)

Date _____   Name _____

Harmonize the following fragments using the principles of block voicing as in the previous worksheets.

1.

2.

3.

4.

5.

Date _____   Name _____

Harmonize in closed-block style.

WORKSHEET 18

Date _____   Name _____

Harmonize in closed-block style. Watch out! All anticipated chords must be handled correctly.

1.

2.

3.
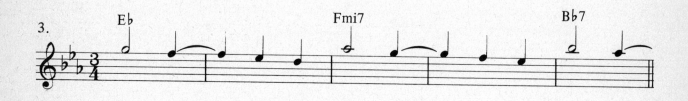

4.

5.

154

Date _____   Name _____

Harmonize in four-part closed-block style. Watch out for the anticipations; they must be handled correctly.

1.

2.

3.

4.

5.

WORKSHEET 20

Date _____   Name _____

Harmonize in four-part closed-block style.

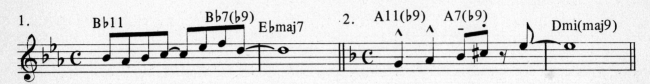

Date _____   Name _____

Harmonize in four-part closed-block style.

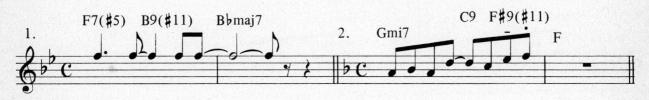

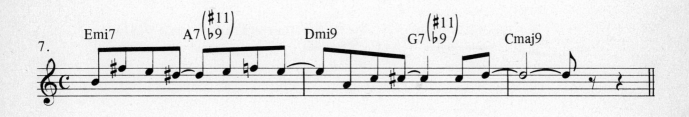

Date _____   Name _____

Harmonize in four-part closed-block style.

Date _____ Name _____

Harmonize in four-part closed-block style.

WORKSHEET 24

Date _____ Name _____

Harmonize in four-part closed-block style.

1.

2.

3.

4.

5.

Date _____ Name _____

Harmonize in four-part closed-block style.

Date _____   Name _____

Harmonize in four-part closed-block style.

Date _____   Name _____

Harmonize in four-part closed-block style.

1.

2.

3.

4.
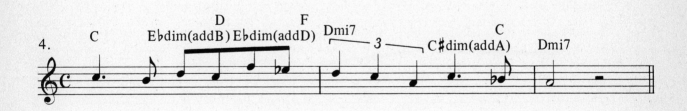

5.
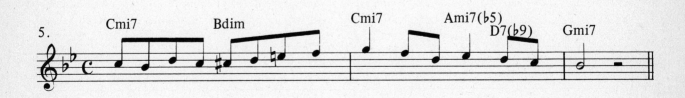

Date _____   Name _____

Harmonize in four-part closed-block style using no repeated notes in lower parts wherever possible.

1.

2.

3.

4.

5.

Date _____   Name _____

Harmonize in four-part closed-block style using no repeated notes in lower parts wherever possible.

WORKSHEET 30

Date _____   Name _____

Harmonize in four-part closed-block style. Use diminished chords for all nonchordal tones, making sure that no parts have repeated notes wherever possible.

1.

2.

3.

4.

5.

Date _____   Name _____

Harmonize in four-part closed-block style. Use diminished chord harmonizations where needed so that all parts move wherever possible.

1.

2.

3.

4.

5.

Date _____   Name _____

Harmonize in four-part closed-block style; use diatonic harmonizations for nonchordal melodic tones, or wherever needed, to provide motion in all parts.

1.

2.

3.

4.

5.

WORKSHEET 33

Date _____   Name _____

Follow the instructions given for Worksheet 32.

Date _____   Name _____

Harmonize in four-part closed-block style, using only the half-step shift for nonchordal tones to provide motion in all parts.

1.

2.

3.

4.

5.

Date _____   Name _____

Harmonize in four-part closed-block style using diminished chords, diatonic chords, or the half-step shift for nonchordal (and sometimes chordal) tones.

1.

2.

3.

4.

5.

Date _____   Name _____

Harmonize using the instructions given for Worksheet 35.

1.

2.

3.

4.

5.

Date _____   Name _____

FOUR-PART BLOCK BLUES

B♭ Trumpet

FOUR-PART BLOCK BLUES

E♭ Alto Sax

Date _____   Name _____

FOUR-PART BLOCK BLUES

B♭ Tenor Sax

FOUR-PART BLOCK BLUES

Trombone

Date _____   Name _____

Articulate the following fragments.

1. Jazz Waltz

2. Rock Ballad

3. Fast Swing

4. Very Slow Swing

5. Moderate Swing

Date _____   Name _____

Articulate the following fragments.

1. Bossa Nova

2. Medium Rock

3. Moderate Swing

4. Fast Swing

5. Samba

Date _____   Name _____

Vary the following fragments using the principles with which we have been dealing in the text. For now, alter only the rhythms; do not add or repeat any notes. Add style and tempo markings.

1.

2.

3.

4.

Date _____   Name _____

Vary the following melodic fragment five different ways by using only rhythmic alterations. Add style and tempo markings.

Original

Date _____   Name _____

Vary the following fragments using only passing tones. For now, do not alter the basic rhythm of the given passages.

1.

2.

3.

4.

Date _____   Name _____

Vary the following fragments using both rhythmic changes and passing tones. Harmonize in four-part block.

1.

2.

3.

4.

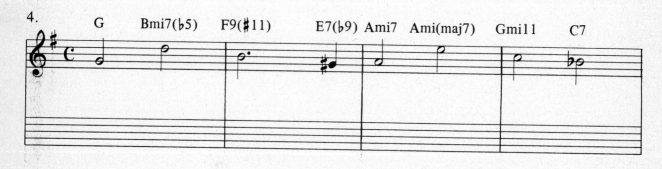

Date _____   Name _____

The following is a simple melodic phrase with chord symbols. Follow the directions for each variaton and harmonize in four-part block.

1. Vary using rhythmic changes and diatonic neighboring tones.

2. Vary using rhythmic changes and single neighboring tones, either diatonic or chromatic.

3. Vary using rhythmic changes and double neighboring tones, either diatonic or chromatic.

4. Vary using any or all embellishment techniques.

5. Vary using any or all embellishment techniques.

Date _____   Name _____

The following is a simple melodic phrase with chord symbols. Follow the directions for each variation and harmonize in four-part block.

1. Vary using rhythmic changes and diatonic neighboring tones.

2. Vary using rhythmic changes and single neighboring tones, either diatonic or chromatic.

3. Vary using rhythmic changes and double neighboring tones, either diatonic or chromatic.

4. Vary using any or all embellishment techniques.

5. Vary using any or all embellishment techniques.

Date _____   Name _____

Arrange an altered version of the following melody using all the devices that we have covered. After this version has been checked by the instructor, harmonize in four-part block, using combinations of open and closed voicing. This tune may be arranged in any style and in any number of different tempos, so be sure to include your own style and tempo markings.

BILL BAILEY

Name

Name _____

Name _____

Date _____   Name _____

BILL BAILEY

Bass

Date _____   Name _____

Write a piano or guitar part for the following fragments; use the several varieties of notation covered in the text.

1. Very Fast Swing

2. Fast Jazz Waltz

3. Medium Latin Rock

4. Slow Swing

Date _____   Name _____

Write rhythm parts for the following harmonized fragments; simplify and condense the chord structures using the principles discussed in the text.

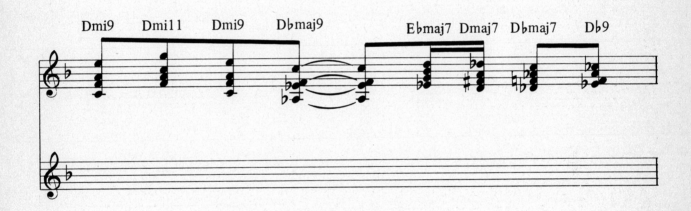

Date _____   Name _____

Write rhythm parts for the following harmonized fragments; simplify the chord structure for a practical piano, guitar, and bass part.

Fast Swing

Date _____   Name _____

BILL BAILEY

Piano/Guitar

Date _____   Name _____

BILL BAILEY

Drums

Date _____   Name _____

1. Embellish the melody in a medium jazz style and tempo.
2. Harmonize for four instruments: trumpet, alto sax, tenor sax, and trombone (or for whatever is available).
3. Write a piano or guitar part and a bass part.
4. Write a drum part.
5. Transpose the front-line parts; copy the bass and drum parts.
6. With a pianist or guitarist playing from the score, play the arrangement.

PENNIES FROM HEAVEN

Johnny Burke
Arthur Johnston

Name _____

Name _____

Name _____

Name _____

Name _____

Date _____   Name _____

Compose introductions based upon the following chord progression in the indicated style and tempo.

G♭maj7   D♭maj7 E♭mi7   Fmi7   B♭7   Ami7   D7   G

Bossa Nova

Slow Swing

Jazz Waltz

Name _____

Medium Rock

Fast Swing

Slow Ballad Tempo

Date _____   Name _____

Compose introductions based upon the following chord progression in the indicated style and tempo.

Eb   C7(b9)   Fmi7   Bb7   Eb   Fmi7   Gmi7   Gb9   Fmi7

5/4 Rock

Medium Swing

Slow Rock Ballad

Name _____

Medium Shuffle

Tango

Ballroom Waltz

Date _____   Name _____

Compose fills for the following melodic fragment where the melody is static. Include
style and tempo markings for each example.

Date _____   Name _____

Compose fills for the following melodic fragments where the melody drops out. Include
style and tempo markings.

Date _____   Name _____

Compose endings for the following example. Use only the chord progression given; include style and tempo markings.

Original

Dmi7 G13(♭9)   C   A♭   Fmi7   B♭9   C

1.

2.

3.

4.

5.

Date _____   Name _____

Compose endings for the following example. Use only the chord progression given; include style and tempo markings for each example.

Original

D7   Emi7   A7   Ami7   D7   G C9 G

1.

2.

3.

4.

5.

Date _____   Name _____

Arrange the following tune for the indicated instruments using all the techniques discussed so far. The melody is arranged in a simplified form so that further rhythmic and melodic changes can be made; the harmonies are not the original but have been altered for added variety. Fills as well as the ending must be composed to the given chord progressions.

We have simplified the score set-up so that piano or guitar plus bass are represented by a single staff.

HAVE YOU MET MISS JONES?

Lorenz Hart
Richard Rodgers

Name _____

Name _____

Name _____

16

17

18

19

20

21

Name _____

Name _____

appendix 1

Date _____   Name _____

A LITTLE BLUES IN FIVE

Andrew Charlton
John M. DeVries

Slow Funky Blues

Date _____   Name _____

SWINGIN' LINE

Andrew Charlton
John M. DeVries

Easy Swing

1   2

3   4

5   6

7   8

9   10

11   12

Name _____

SWINGIN' LINE

216

Date _____   Name _____

WALTZ FOR KATHIE

Andrew Charlton
John M. DeVries

Medium Waltz Tempo or Fast Jazz Waltz

217

Name _____

WALTZ FOR KATHIE

218

Date _____   Name _____

WALKIN' EASY

Andrew Charlton
John M. DeVries

Medium Swing

219

Name _____

WALKIN' EASY

Date _____   Name _____

ANOTHER TIME

John M. DeVries
Andrew Charlton

Ballad Tempo

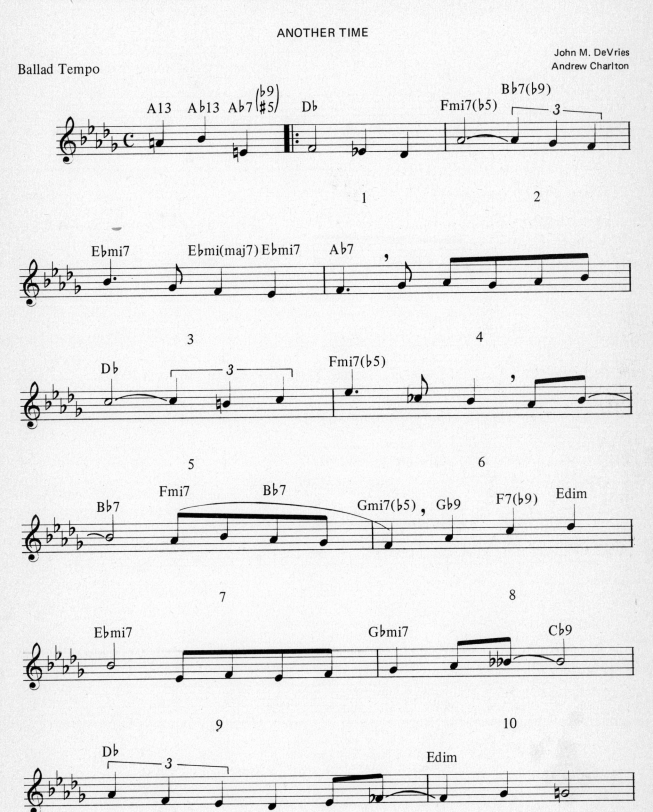

Name _____

ANOTHER TIME

222

Date _____   Name _____

SENTIMENTAL BALLAD

Andrew Charlton
John M. DeVries

Medium Ballad Tempo

Name _____

SENTIMENTAL BALLAD

appendix 2

SENTIMENTAL BALLAD

Andrew Charlton
John M. DeVries

Choose a style and tempo

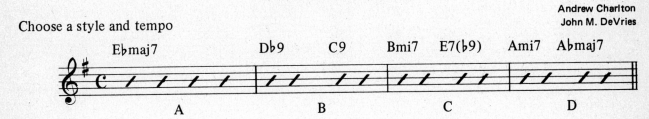

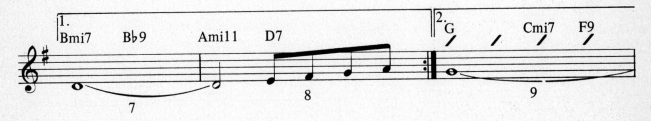

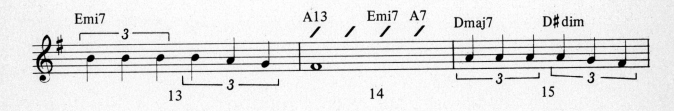

SENTIMENTAL BALLAD

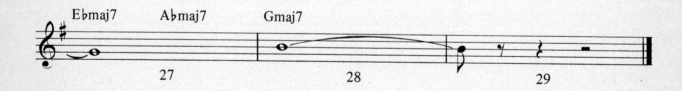

SWEETPEA

Andrew Charlton
John M. DeVries

Choose a style and tempo

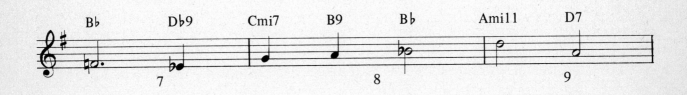

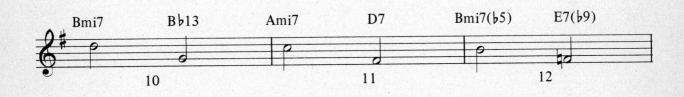

SWEETPEA

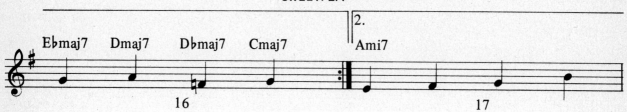

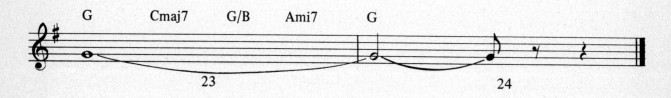

The way in which this tune is constructed is rather simple. You must make extensive alterations in the rhythm as well as in the melody to make it into a workable style.

SOMETHIN' HAPPY

Andrew Charlton
John M. DeVries

Choose a style and tempo

SOMETHIN' HAPPY

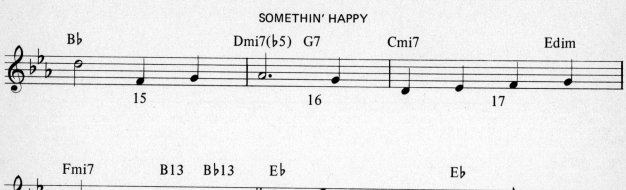

HERE YOU ARE

Andrew Charlton
John M. DeVries

Choose a style and tempo

HERE YOU ARE

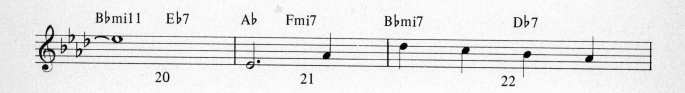

GOT NO BLUES

Andrew Charlton
John M. DeVries

Choose a style and tempo

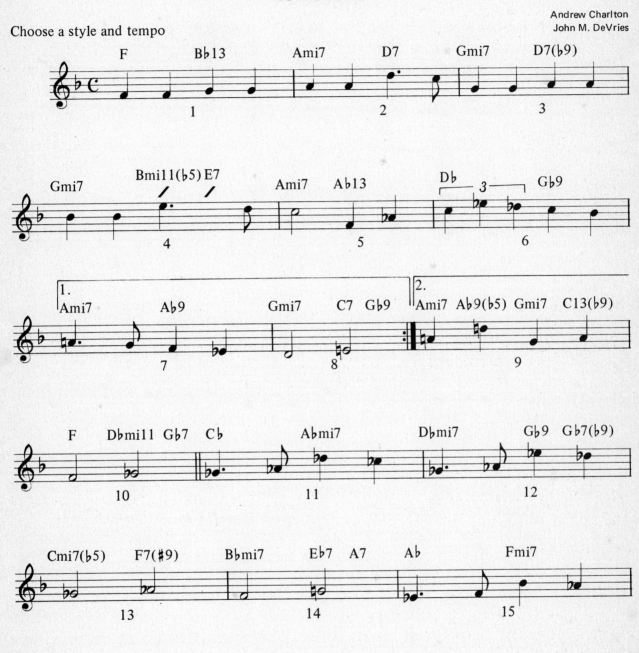

GOT NO BLUES